How to Grow an Opportunity Tree

Follow the Path, Live the Dream

The Ultimate Investment Part 2

A Business Fable

By H. Bradley Stucki

See other works by H. Bradley Stucki at www.amazon.com/author/hbstucki. Free downloads are often available. Also, click "Follow" on his Author Page to be notified of new releases.

Chapter One

One year had passed for the Benjamin family.

Dan stood in the hallway of their small two-story home, looking at the family portrait the way he'd done on the night this all began—and on the morning everything had changed. The faces in the portrait hadn't aged. His had. At forty-seven, his brown hair was going gray, and he carried more weight around his middle than he cared to admit.

But that wasn't why he was standing here. He was standing here because he didn't know how to walk into the kitchen and say what he had to say.

The envelope was in his hand. He'd read it in the parking lot, sitting in the car, and then he'd driven home in silence, the way he'd once driven home the night Frank laid him off. That felt like a lifetime ago. He and Mandie had found the Ultimate Investment since then. They'd met Elizabeth. They'd read her letter on the couch. They'd planned at the kitchen table. They'd said "It's time" and meant it.

And now this.

He could hear Mandie in the kitchen. She'd taken a break from her online coursework—the business management program she'd started the year before, the one that had already changed how she thought about their finances, their planning, everything. Her laptop was probably open on the counter, the way it usually was.

On the refrigerator hung a small wooden plaque Mandie had made—hand-lettered and painted, mounted at eye level. She'd crafted it not long after she'd folded the original paper note into

Dan's wallet, wanting her own daily reminder in the heart of the house. Seven words in her careful hand:

Invest your time. Don't just spend it.

Dan looked at the portrait one more time. Then he walked into the kitchen.

"Dan?" Mandie looked up from the counter where she'd been reviewing their monthly budget—a habit she'd developed from her coursework. She saw his face and her hands went still. "What happened?"

"It's Contra Pro." He set the envelope on the counter between them. "They're done, Mandie."

She picked it up and read. He watched her face—the furrow deepening, the jaw tightening—and he could tell exactly which paragraph she'd reached by the way her expression changed.

"Bankrupt," she said.

"Jake couldn't get the software working. Not reliably enough to ship. They burned through the capital trying, and the investors pulled out. Barney called me this morning before the letter arrived. He was—" Dan paused, remembering the sound of Barney's voice on the phone—hoarse, ashamed, barely holding together. "He was devastated. He kept apologizing. He said they'd tried everything."

"I believe him," Mandie said quietly. She set the letter down. "I watched Jake work on that software for nine months. He never stopped trying. The bugs were real, Dan. The product just wasn't ready."

"It doesn't matter now. The company's dissolving. There's no final paycheck. The commissions we were counting on—"

"Gone."

"Gone."

The kitchen was quiet. The refrigerator hummed. The plaque on its door caught the light.

"What about unemployment?" Mandie asked. She'd already shifted—he could see it happening, the way she moved from grief to calculation. Her coursework had done that. She thought in systems now. "Your base pay was the stipend, not commissions. That's what they'll calculate from."

"I stopped by on the way home. It's minimal. Barely covers food and utilities."

"What about the house payment?" Mandie's voice was steady but he could hear the effort it took to keep it that way. "We used most of our savings getting through last year. The 401k is gone. We borrowed against your life insurance."

"I know." Dan pulled out a chair and sat down heavily. "I don't have an answer for the house yet."

Mandie sat across from him. She didn't reach for his hand— not yet. She was still processing, still running numbers in her head the way she did now.

"This one felt different, Dan. This one felt real."

"It was real. That's what makes it worse. Barney and Jake weren't liars. They weren't running a scam. They just... couldn't get there. The product wasn't ready, and they ran out of time and money before it was."

He thought of Elizabeth's letter, folded in the drawer of the end table six feet away. *You receive it new each morning. You cannot save it, buy more of it, or get it back once it's gone.* Contra Pro had run out of time. The irony was almost unbearable.

"I'm so sorry," Dan said. "I'm sorry to put you and the kids through this again."

Mandie looked at him for a long moment. Then she reached across the table and took his hands.

"We made this decision together. At the kitchen table. In the lamplight. Remember? I said 'Then we do it.' I said 'Partners.' I meant it then and I mean it now. This isn't your failure, Dan. It's our setback. And we'll figure it out the way we've figured out everything else—together."

Dan looked at his wife—the woman who had tracked down E.M.A., who had heard what Elizabeth wasn't saying, who had kissed a dying woman's cheek and kept a promise to watch over him. Who had studied and grown and become someone neither of them had expected. Who was already, he could see, thinking three steps ahead.

"I don't deserve you," he said.

"You absolutely don't," she said. And then she almost smiled. "But you're stuck with me. Now. Let me get my folder. We need to look at the numbers."

She stood and crossed to the counter where her manila folder sat—the same folder that had started as a detective's file hunting for

E.M.A. and was now thick with budgets, coursework notes, and their financial planning. She brought it back to the table, opened it, and clicked her pen.

"First things first," she said. "What do we have, and how long does it last?"

Chapter Two

The next day was Friday. After a full day of pounding the pavement looking for work, Dan sat at the desk he'd set up in their small front room as a home office. He'd created the space so he could spend more time at home after starting his now-defunct job. Leaning back in his swivel chair, he ran his fingers through his still-thick, though graying brown hair. The stress was overwhelming. No matter what he did, things never seemed to work out for him and his family.

He'd thought he'd finally figured it all out when he learned the secret of The Ultimate Investment. But that investment hadn't delivered as they'd hoped. Now he was behind the proverbial eight ball... again.

The unemployment benefits wouldn't cover their basic expenses, and their savings and 401k were depleted. They'd even borrowed against his life insurance policy while waiting for the big payday from the new company.

Which bills could they skip this time? He hated having his family live like this. The three kids – 14-year-old Dan Jr., 12-year-old Melissa, and 9-year-old Ronnie – had noticed the change despite his and Mandie's attempts to hide it. They seemed subdued and afraid to speak up. Even Moochie, the family dog, was giving him a wide berth. Mandie probably had a hand in that, ensuring the kids gave him space to sort his job search.

Mandie never criticized, though he knew she felt the strain too – perhaps more than he did – and tried to hide it for his sake. She was truly precious. He couldn't fathom what he'd done to deserve her. Dan needed to do right by her and the kids.

They had already sacrificed more than enough while he tried to "get ahead," only to have another job dissolve. Despite the long hours and hard work, success always seemed to hover just over the next hill, never quite within reach. He must be cursed.

Dan had been certain that once he'd finally learned the secret of The Ultimate Investment, his life would change. Well, it had changed – just not in the way he'd hoped. He remained unemployed. Though he knew the secret and had a plan to use it wisely, he felt stymied and lost. The plan wasn't doing him any good. He felt trapped behind an impenetrable wall.

"Dinner, dear?" Mandie called from the kitchen. "The kids have eaten and are outside playing."

Dan started. How had he missed dinner?

Mandie approached his makeshift office space in the living room.

"You looked so intense, I thought it best not to disturb you," she said with a gentle smile. She'd been at the kitchen table with her laptop—her coursework, probably, or the budget spreadsheet she'd been refining. She'd closed it before she came to him.

Dan caught her hand and drew her close, wrapping his arm around her waist. "You're way too good for me, you know that?"

"Of course, I know," Mandie said. "You married above yourself. And until I get you properly trained, I can't trade you in for much."

"You've got that right," Dan said, only half-joking.

"Come on, dear. You know I'm teasing."

"I know. But I'm not. You and the kids deserve so much more. If I only knew what I was doing wrong, I'd do things differently."

"You know it takes *time*," Mandie said, emphasizing the last word. "Things will work out. You need to let them take their course."

"That's the problem," Dan said, tension creeping into his voice despite his efforts to suppress it. "I can't see that course. I feel like a sprinter running in circles without a finish line. I'm like an archer without a target. The bow is drawn back, all the tension is there, but there's nothing to shoot at."

"We can tell you've been tense," Mandie smiled, draping an arm around his shoulders and kissing the top of his head. "Anything I can do to help with that?"

Dan's eyes twinkled and his smile widened.

"Like talking things through?" Mandie's knowing smile deepened. "Remember, I'm a partner in this too. You don't have to shoulder it all alone."

"But you've already got so much on your plate—the coursework, the kids, managing the house and our finances. I don't want to pile more on you."

"I'm not talking about getting a job yet," Mandie said. "Remember how we worked together to find The Ultimate Investment? I can help you find your – *our* – course. If we set the course together, we can work on it together. You won't have to carry the whole load. I might see something you can't because you're too *tense*." Again, that gentle smile played across her face.

"That's true," Dan admitted. They had worked well together then. He loved how Mandie had been just as committed to discovering The Ultimate Investment as he had been. It was a time when they'd truly collaborated on something important, when they'd been closest. He realized he'd withdrawn into himself again. Mandie had worried he would have a midlife crisis like her Uncle Will.

Dan gazed deeply into Mandie's eyes. Though she maintained a brave face, he could see the worry lurking beneath.

"I know. I just keep underestimating you. You'd think I'd learn."

"Listen!" Mandie said. "We're partners. You said it yourself. And we made an agreement that you wouldn't make any major decisions without discussing them with me."

"I wish I had some major decisions we could talk about," Dan said.

"We do," Mandie insisted. "A direction to go in, remember? That target? I think we should work on that together. Setting a target to shoot for will help you focus on where we can make the most of *our* Ultimate Investment."

The tension Dan had been carrying began to ease as he considered Mandie's words. He'd wanted to talk with her but had worried she'd think he was being unrealistic. He realized he'd underestimated her... again.

"Why do you put up with my failures?" Dan finally voiced his deepest fear. "I've let you down not once, but twice."

"You haven't let me down!" Mandie declared. "I've watched you leave this house every morning and work hard to put food on our table. It would be different if you weren't trying your best. I know if you put that same effort into the next job, it will pay off."

"Come on," Mandie said. "Let's get you fed. We'll figure this out tomorrow. Remember those meeting rooms at the Library? We'll call it our first board meeting. Tomorrow's Saturday. The kids have been wanting to visit their cousins. I'll arrange that while you eat."

Mandie pulled him up from his chair. As he stood, he embraced her warmly. "You did marry beneath yourself, but I'm so grateful you did."

Chapter Three

The library's meeting room felt familiar—the same room where they'd once searched for Elizabeth's clues, where they'd first said the word "time" aloud and felt the world shift. Mandie had her manila folder open on the table, a fresh page of notes beside a printout she'd made that morning.

"I ran the numbers last night," she said. "Here's where we stand." She slid the printout toward Dan. "Unemployment covers about forty percent of our monthly obligations. Our remaining savings—what's left after the life insurance loan—gives us roughly eight weeks of runway before we start missing payments."

Dan studied the figures. They were clean, precise—her coursework showing in every column. "Eight weeks," he said.

"Eight weeks," she confirmed. "Which means we have two choices, and they're not really either-or. They're both."

She'd already written them on the legal pad. Dan read them upside down across the table:

"One: you find a job as fast as possible. Any job that brings in income. That stabilizes us. Two: while you're working, we invest whatever time we can into building something on the side— something that could eventually become a living we actually want, not just one we're surviving on."

"Both at once," Dan said.

"Both at once. The job keeps us afloat. The Ultimate Investment builds something underneath us while we're treading water."

Dan leaned back in his chair. The logic was clean. The problem was that it assumed he could find a job, and so far the market had given him nothing but silence.

"I know what you're thinking," Mandie said. "The job market is terrible. But the numbers don't care about the market. We need income in eight weeks or we start falling behind on the house. So we work the problem from both ends—you search for work while we figure out what the 'something on the side' might be."

"And the second part?" Dan asked. "The something on the side? We don't even know what that looks like yet."

"No," Mandie agreed. "But we know the principle. Elizabeth's letter said invest your time in what you love. Sheldon showed it by doing. We don't have to know the 'what' yet—we just have to keep our eyes open for it while we handle the immediate crisis."

Dan nodded slowly. The decision was logical, practical, and he knew it was right. Still, the thought of starting over again weighed heavily. He reached across the table and took Mandie's hand.

"Eight weeks," he said.

"Eight weeks," she said. "We've worked with less."

She clicked her pen, turned to a fresh page, and wrote at the top: "Week One."

Chapter Four

Three weeks had passed.

Dan lay in bed, his thoughts racing. He'd never missed a house payment before, and the reality was eating away at him. The clock radio's red digits showed 2:00 AM – another sleepless night. This pattern couldn't continue without affecting his health. He glanced at Mandie, her breathing soft and steady. Getting up risked waking her, but lying here counting sheep seemed futile. Dwelling on their situation would only make him more restless. There had to be a way to quiet his mind enough for sleep. Without rest, he'd be useless at job hunting tomorrow. Did that even matter? He was just spinning his wheels anyway. No! He couldn't think like that. There had to be a solution, and he would find it!

Eyes squeezed shut, he tried focusing on something else. He'd read that visualizing a peaceful setting – like sitting on a sunny beach with rolling waves – could induce relaxation. Dan tried: A sunny beach... Nothing. It wasn't working.

What else could he do? He'd also read that listing your worries and planning how to address them could ease anxiety enough for sleep. Since the beach visualization had failed, he might as well try making that list. Who knew? Maybe this restlessness was a sign that answers would soon emerge.

His mind was racing, thoughts tumbling over each other. It amazed him that he'd maintained his sanity. Here he was, in another stretch without a job or purpose to occupy his mind and energy. Now his life seemed to mirror his thoughts: aimless, urgent, and stress-filled.

Carefully rolling off the bed to minimize movement, Dan stood and crept out the door, gently pulling it closed behind him. He paused, listening to Mandie's even breathing. Good – he hadn't disturbed her. She needed rest as much as he did, perhaps more given her ongoing responsibilities with the kids and home.

He moved silently through the hallway and down the stairs, mindful not to wake the children. Though they usually slept like rocks – making mornings a challenge – he didn't want to risk disturbing their peace.

In the front room, Dan settled at his desk and switched on a small lamp, creating a pool of light on the desktop. He pulled out a legal pad and stared at its blank expanse. Nothing came. He was willing to work hard, to do whatever it took. The problem lay in the scarcity of opportunities. Dan had struck out everywhere. The local defense contractor, Synodyne, had implemented massive layoffs after losing their largest contract several months ago, and those displaced workers had quickly claimed every available position in the area. No one was hiring.

Usually, sales jobs were plentiful, especially for someone with Dan's solid track record. But something felt different now.

The idea of starting his own business crept back into his thoughts. Perhaps that was his only option. His recent venture had resembled entrepreneurship – they'd provided subsistence pay, a stake in the company, and promises of substantial bonuses once the product shipped. Still, it hadn't truly been his own. He'd been more of a glorified employee, sharing both risk and potential rewards. In the end, the risk had crushed him.

Besides, they'd already discussed this path. They lacked both the time for him to build a business and the start-up sacrifices, having invested that in their last "opportunity." They needed steady income now!

Yet if he did start his own business, what would it be? Nothing sparked particular passion. He could purchase an existing business, but that would mean taking on more debt, and they had no down payment. Mandie would likely oppose that idea anyway.

Dan shook his head and stared at the blank paper. *So much for writing things down. Considering what to write is only making everything worse.* Besides, Mandie had insisted they tackle this together. Maybe she had insights he couldn't see. Her ideas would certainly be as good as his. Usually better.

No matter which direction his thoughts took, they always led him in circles. He should get a job – but there were no jobs. He could start a business – but what kind, and how would they survive while building it? He could buy a business – but how, without cash? Financing might work, but they'd need a down payment, which they didn't have.

"Aaarh!" Dan thumped his head on the desk, careful to keep the sound muffled.

He switched off the light and moved to the couch. The house's silence felt deafening. A beam of street light pierced through the blinds, casting a trapezoid on the floor. Dan stared at it, his eyes growing heavy. They closed, blinked open, then closed again. As he drifted off, he began to dream...

Chapter Five

Dan's Dream:

Dawn painted the sky in soft golden hues as Dan stood at the edge of a broad grassy meadow. Behind him rose a line of rocky cliffs, dotted with stubby pines and towering cactus. A gentle breeze stirred the tails of his white dress shirt. He was wearing jeans. He turned to face the cliffs. With his first step, he realized he was barefoot. His windblown hair and unusual attire made him feel strangely vulnerable.

Looking down, he discovered he stood at the beginning of a path. His eyes followed its course into a narrow pass cut through the cliffs, the trail disappearing into shadow between vertical rock walls that curved out of sight.

Something deep within urged him to follow the path. He moved into the mouth of the cliffs, continuing around a gentle bend until a narrow box canyon opened before him, stretching roughly three hundred yards into the distance.

There, perched majestically upon a rise at the canyon's end, stood a magnificent tree. It towered at least a hundred feet high, its branches spanning the width of the gorge. Thick, vibrant green leaves danced in the breeze, and even from this distance he could see golden fruit weighing down each branch.

Dan felt an overwhelming desire to reach the tree and taste its fruit. Something within told him it would be incomparably delicious—that if he could only reach the tree, he would experience joy beyond description.

The path wound gently through the canyon, eventually climbing a steep incline to the level ground where the tree grew.

Along the way, branching byways and side trails disappeared behind massive boulders and into fissures in the canyon walls. The canyon floor was a maze of boulders, sagebrush, flowering cactus, and tall tamarisk trees. Yet the great tree remained visible above it all, beckoning him forward.

He wasn't alone. People wandered among the boulders and brush, searching for something they couldn't seem to find. They kept their heads down, refusing to look up. Dan felt compelled to call out, to point to the tree. But he remained silent, fearing his voice might shatter the dream. Something told him this vision was important.

I think I'm dreaming.

Yet the realization didn't diminish his desire. He kept his gaze fixed on the tree and moved up the path.

Halfway through, a side trail caught his eye. Behind a massive boulder he glimpsed an enchanting bush whose branches sparkled with what appeared to be diamonds and golden bangles. The dazzling wealth seemed greater than the tree's, more accessible, easier to reach.

Dan hesitated. Then he caught himself. No. This wasn't what he truly sought. His heart yearned for the promise that drew him to the tree. He turned back to the path. The pull seemed even stronger now, as if his sacrifice had intensified it.

The path soon led downward into a depression, overgrown with larger bushes and squat pines, strewn with rocks that made walking difficult, especially barefoot. The light dimmed, and the way took on a gloomy aspect. Dan could no longer see the tree ahead or the progress he'd made behind him. All he could do was trust the path and keep moving.

Eventually the path climbed again, and he stopped at the foot of the final steep incline. He could see the tree's branches and fruit from where he stood. They seemed to glow as they swayed in the breeze, their movement almost hypnotic. He was so close.

The last thirty feet rose steeply. Dan climbed cautiously, using his hands for balance, knowing a slip would send him sliding back. At last he reached the top, breathless. He crossed the level, grassy ground to the foot of the tree. Its limbs swayed gently and its leaves rustled in the slight breeze, emanating a warmth he felt in his soul.

This is so right.

He turned to take in the view. Many people still wandered the canyon floor, lost and searching. A handful were making their way up the path. Then Dan noticed a man in a small boat, gliding down a branch of the creek from higher in the canyon to the base of the rise. The man disembarked, reached up, plucked one of the golden fruits, and took a bite. He chewed briefly, shrugged as if wondering what all the fuss was about, dropped the fruit on the ground, returned to his boat, and let it drift with the stream down into the canyon.

Others who had climbed the path were biting into the fruit. Their faces beamed with sublime radiance, as if they had discovered what they'd sought their entire lives. Tears streamed down their faces as they laughed and cried and embraced one another.

That's what I want.

Dan moved to a branch and reached up to pluck a glistening, golden fruit. It resembled a cross between a pear and an apple. His teeth pierced the skin, and juice flowed into his mouth. A feeling of euphoria spread through his entire body. Such contentment, such satisfaction! It spread through him in undulating waves that caressed and burned and tingled all at once.

He staggered with the sensation. The warmth pervaded his being. He took another bite. The second taste didn't diminish the experience in the slightest.

I wish I could feel this way always.

Then an idea struck him. Dan carefully plucked three more fruits from his branch. No one objected. He cradled them gently and took one final look over the rise, committing everything to memory—the sights, the feelings. He would want to remember this when he woke.

The descent proved much easier than the climb. He followed the path back through the canyon, the side trails holding no attraction now. He passed them easily, offering encouraging smiles to those he met along the path, until he strode out onto the plain of tall meadow grasses.

Dan walked until he came to a slight rise. Here he stopped and broke open the golden fruit. He bit into it, and the euphoria returned, undimmed by distance from the mother tree. Great relief washed over him.

With great care, he extracted the seeds from each piece of fruit. He tucked most into his pocket, but kept three in his palm. Using his free hand, he cleared a small circle of grass and dug into the rich, loamy soil beneath. Into this hole he placed the three seeds, covering them with gentle attention.

Time passed—and Dan marveled at its swift flow, this being a dream—as he nourished, groomed, and tended the sprouting tree with dedication. He pruned, watered, and carefully tended the soil, encouraging his tree to flourish.

And flourish it did, growing to rival the original. Dan knew he had created something he could partake of for the rest of his life. Even without the fruit, he felt tremendous joy and satisfaction from completing this labor of love.

It was all he'd ever wanted, and he'd done it.

Chapter Six

"Dan... Dan, wake up." A gentle nudge on his arm jolted him awake, and he looked up through bleary eyes into Mandie's concerned face. "You fell asleep on the couch."

As he stretched and sat up, the memory flooded back...

"Can't talk now, hon," Dan said, jumping to his feet. "I've got to get this down." Leaving a stunned Mandie standing open-mouthed, he strode to his desk, grabbed the scratch pad and pen from the night before, and hurried up the stairs to the bedroom. Dan knew the kids would be up soon, and he needed quiet to record the dream he'd just experienced. Mandie would understand once he showed it to her.

Dan sat on the bed, switched on the nightstand lamp, and began writing. He didn't stop until he had captured every detail.

#

"Here we are," Dan said to Mandie as they stepped into the quiet conference room of their local library.

After finishing his dream account, he'd gone back downstairs and helped Mandie with the dishes. Once the kids had left for school, Dan had asked Mandie if they could talk. She readily agreed, and they'd come to the library as soon as it opened. Dan had suggested the location, remembering their previous breakthroughs there.

"I'm sorry about this morning," Dan said, holding a chair for Mandie before taking his own seat. "I had a dream last night and needed to write it down before I lost any details. Here, take a look."

He withdrew the folded sheets from his pocket and handed them to her.

Dan remained quiet as Mandie read, not wanting to break her concentration. The dream felt as significant as their discovery of "The Ultimate Investment." Somehow, the dream and those principles seemed to fit together in a crucial way.

He smiled wryly to himself. *Strange to have these feelings when everything is falling apart. Maybe I'm just grasping at straws.*

That's why Mandie's opinion and counsel were so vital. She was the smart one, after all.

"Wow," was all Mandie said when she finished reading. "What do you think it means?"

Dan considered his words carefully. "It has a lot to do with what we're going through. I feel like I need to find that path and stick with it. I'll find that tree and taste that fruit, and then..." He paused. "I know I was alone in the dream, but I have a feeling what I experienced was meant for all of us."

Mandie fell silent. He could see her processing the information. Dan waited patiently, knowing her perspective was crucial.

"I agree," she finally said. "I think you had this dream for a reason. I also think that following the path is key. But what path? How will you know when you find it?"

"Good question," Dan said, relieved that Mandie wasn't dismissing his experience as foolish. Of course, he had no clear direction yet. Still, having her support was essential, just as she'd said. He wouldn't make the mistake of excluding her again.

They both fell quiet.

"What are you thinking?" Mandie asked.

"I'm wondering about the next step," Dan answered. "We've discussed many things, but the most urgent is ensuring we can pay our bills. The best and quickest way is for me to get another job. Any job. Once I do that, I'll feel more comfortable exploring other options. I'll use 'The Ultimate Investment' to build those other options when we can afford to consider them."

"There's a saying," Mandie said, taking Dan's hand, "When a student is ready, a teacher will appear."

"Well, this student is certainly ready," Dan said.

"If we keep your dream in mind and stay alert, understanding will come with time. It's like the path in your dream. Sometimes you couldn't see the tree, but you knew if you stayed on course, you'd reach it."

Mandie paused, and Dan noticed tears glistening in her eyes. "I think you... we... just stepped onto the path."

Chapter Seven

One month later.

"Hi, Honey, I'm home," Dan called out as he stepped through the front door and began loosening his tie.

"I'm in here," Mandie responded from the kitchen.

Dan walked in and gave her a warm hug and lingering kiss.

"That's quite a kiss," Mandie said. "Any special occasion?"

"I wish," Dan said. "I've been pounding the pavement all day. I'm up to seventy-five applications now. Tomorrow I'll switch to following up. I read somewhere it takes three follow-up calls after submitting an application to get an interview."

"You're keeping track?"

"May as well. Seems like the right thing to do. Would you mind if I spend some time in the garage before dinner working on Dan Jr.'s birthday gift like we discussed?"

"Perfect timing. The kids just got home and are playing out back with some friends. They'll be occupied. I'll keep them away from the garage."

"Thanks," Dan said, hugging Mandie again. "I'll change and get started."

#

Dan sat at his workbench in the garage, contemplating his next steps. It had been ages since he'd worked here, and truthfully, he welcomed the opportunity to return to it.

His father had introduced him to fine metalworking in his teens. Dan had discovered a natural aptitude for it and taken every shop class available in high school. He remembered losing himself for hours in his work with metals, creating sculptures and intricate puzzles.

During his final few Christmases at home, his father had asked him to create the family's gifts for neighbors. Dan had designed simple puzzles from heavy-gauge wire, soldering pieces together with moving parts. Though modest creations, they'd always delighted recipients. Dan had loved both the work itself and the joy it brought others.

Then came college, marriage, and career obligations. He'd set the hobby aside. Now it would serve a purpose again.

Christmas lay six months ahead, but more immediately, Dan Jr.'s birthday approached next week. To economize, he and Mandie had decided he would create handmade gifts for both birthdays and Christmas.

Dan had gathered his materials: heavy-gauge wire, soldering iron, cutters, and an assortment of spare nuts, bolts, and washers. He'd arranged them on the workbench he'd built at the garage's front, positioning a shop light for proper illumination.

"Now comes the Creation," Dan muttered, rubbing his hands together like an enthusiastic inventor.

He'd been planning this piece carefully. Danny excelled at soccer, standing out as one of his team's strongest players. Dan had finally witnessed his son's matches... because he was unemployed.

Don't dwell on that now, Dan thought. *Focus on creating*. He'd decided on a wire sculpture depicting a soccer player mid-kick. Though simple in design, it would be unique. He hoped Danny would appreciate it.

As Dan began working, he slipped into that familiar creative zone he remembered so well. A dreamy contentment settled over him as he lost himself in the process. Though it felt like hours, only forty-five minutes passed before he attached the figurine to an inexpensive black plastic base from the hardware store. He held it up, examining every detail to ensure perfection. After a moment's consideration, he took a screwdriver and made a tiny etch on the figurine's right foot – barely noticeable.

"To symbolize being on the path," he whispered. He held the figurine up and studied it, turning it slowly in the light. Something stirred in his memory—Elizabeth's story of Sheldon, showing up at six in the morning with two thermoses of coffee, filling a notebook with careful observations about wobbling tables and sticking needles. Looking at a thing carefully and wanting to make it better. Dan glanced at the wire and solder on his workbench, at the small sculpture in his hands. He didn't know yet what any of this meant. But the feeling was right.

The final touch was engraving the small plate: *World's Greatest Soccer Kid.*

"Dan, supper's ready."

He started, having been so focused on positioning the plate that he hadn't heard Mandie enter.

"Wow, you finished already?"

"What do you think?" Dan held up the figurine for her inspection.

"It's perfect!"

Dan glowed at her sincere praise.

"You couldn't find anything like this in stores. Danny will love it!"

"Would similar pieces work for Christmas gifts?"

"Absolutely. The neighbors will be relieved they're not getting cocoa cans with bows this year. Now come on, the kids are getting restless, and I don't want to leave them alone with the food too long."

Dan placed the figurine on a high shelf, out of sight. Mandie winked, letting him know she'd remember its location for wrapping later. Then, arm in arm, they returned to the kitchen and some much-needed family time.

#

Dan sat in yet another waiting room, facing another application to complete. Six months into his job search, he still hadn't secured a second interview. The response was always the same: "We wish we were hiring because you're just the person we'd be looking for, but we're full up..."

His attention drifted to the coffee table, where a magazine called "Local Entrepreneur" caught his eye. The cover featured a familiar face from the Chamber of Commerce, with the headline "Blaine's Wonderful World of Bunnies." Intrigued, he picked it up and began reading.

The article detailed how Blaine Kreskin had built an extraordinary career selling fluffy stuffed bunnies. Known as the Fluffy Bunny Magnate, he distributed his plush creations worldwide from his local warehouse.

A quote from Blaine jumped off the page: "The object of life is to love what you're doing and to serve others."

That's it exactly! Dan thought, his mind immediately connecting to his dream and the delicious fruit.

That feeling must be what Blaine's talking about. He's found his own tree, his own opportunity to live the dream. I've got to learn how he did it!

Almost without thinking, Dan pulled out his cell phone and called the Chamber of Commerce. A friend there owed him a favor, and soon he had Blaine's number.

Minutes later: "Sure Dan, love to meet with you. How's tomorrow at 2:00 PM?"

Dan caught himself. What had he just done? Though impulsive, it felt right. Well, he had the appointment now. He had the time. It couldn't hurt, and who knew? Maybe Blaine was hiring.

Chapter Eight

"Come in, Dan. How's it going?"

"You don't want to know," Dan replied, settling into an overstuffed chair in Blaine's spacious office. The room was strategically decorated with fluffy stuffed bunnies in every color imaginable – pink, blue, purple, yellow, orange, yellow, red and green. Blaine took a seat across from him and smiled as Dan surveyed the scene.

"Much better than a stuffy showroom," Blaine said. "It lets my customers know I'm passionate about what I do."

"That's the message I get," Dan said, still taking in the unique environment. "Thanks for meeting with me."

"Always glad to meet a fellow Chamber member. What's this I wouldn't want to know?"

"Sorry for the sarcasm," Dan said. "I hope I'm not imposing, but I'm seeking advice. I saw your article in Local Entrepreneur and was struck by your quote: 'The object of life is to love what you're doing and to serve others.' You clearly practice what you preach. I want to understand what you mean by that and how I might achieve it too."

Blaine studied Dan silently for a moment. "Okay, I'll tell you, but first, what really brought you here?"

Dan considered his response, briefly tempted to craft a face-saving story, then decided on honest vulnerability.

"My company just went under, and I'm job hunting. But beyond that, I'm searching for something more meaningful than just a paycheck. I'm looking for..." Dan trailed off, unable to articulate his deeper yearning. He certainly couldn't describe his dream – that would sound absurd.

"Okay. I think I understand," Blaine said. "You want to achieve what I mentioned – to love what you do and serve others."

"Exactly!" Dan exclaimed. "How did you figure it out? You obviously have."

"I'll share my insight," Blaine said, leaning forward in his chair, hands clasped before him, arms resting on his knees. "But I'll warn you – it sounds simple, but it's challenging to execute."

Dan nodded in recognition. "The Ultimate Investment" followed the same pattern. Simple in principle, but requiring discipline, work... and TIME.

"I understand that," Dan said.

Blaine studied Dan, then nodded. "I believe you do. I'll tell you then. Feel free to share it with others, though it probably won't resonate until they're ready to hear it."

Dan immediately recalled Mandie's quote of the ancient Chinese proverb: "When the student is ready, a teacher will appear." It was happening to him! Mandie would be delighted to hear this.

Blaine rose and began pacing. "Mind if I walk while we talk? I think better this way. Stay seated – just bear with me."

"Fine by me," Dan replied, settling back.

"It begins with releasing yourself from others' expectations," Blaine began. "This journey is deeply personal. You can't undertake it while carrying the weight of others' opinions. You need to shed that burden. You must remain open to all possibilities. Look around – when I started, no one would have associated me with 'fluffy bunnies,' myself included."

He paused, looking at Dan. "You understand?"

"I think so," Dan said, his mind wrestling with the concept. "What about my wife? I depend on her insight, and I don't want to disappoint her. I can ignore others' opinions, but my wife and I have an agreement – we don't move forward unless we both feel good about it."

"Hmm," Blaine mused. "Is she supportive?"

"Very," Dan responded quickly. "I want her to be part of this journey."

"That's actually perfect," Blaine said. "She sounds similar to my Sheila. You have an advantage there.

"The key is to involve her completely – share everything so she understands and can be your counselor, advocate, and partner."

"She already is," Dan affirmed.

"Good," Blaine said, resuming his pacing. "Then keep her fully informed of your thoughts and feelings, and share what you're trying to accomplish. She'll support you if she knows the end goal is to 'love what you do and serve others'... while earning a comfortable living. Remember, when you serve others, compensation always follows in some form.

"The first step is learning to recognize great opportunities – they appear constantly. You just need to identify which ones are right for you."

"That's the challenge," Dan said. "How did you know fluffy bunnies were your path?"

"That's not the point," Blaine countered. "It's unique for everyone. Here – I think you're ready for this. I don't share this with just anyone."

Blaine moved to his desk and retrieved a laminated sheet from his top drawer. He handed it to Dan. "I keep this handy as a reminder, even now. Read it later. It's my tool for identifying opportunities that fit me. I'm involved in various ventures besides fluffy bunnies, you know. The document is self-explanatory."

Blaine settled into the chair opposite Dan and leaned forward. "You might not recognize your opportunity immediately. It's often something you do unconsciously, something you lose yourself in but haven't considered as a livelihood – like fluffy bunnies. You'll need to discover it through reflection. It varies for everyone, sometimes surprisingly." He gestured around the room. "That's why I created the guide. It will help you find what's right for you.

"Once you understand how your passion can serve others, you've found your answer! As I said before, service always brings rewards."

Dan nodded. "I think I understand."

Blaine smiled. "Your expression suggests you do."

<u>Blaine's Sheet</u> - Shared with Mandie

Main Objective: Do what you love and serve others.

Unearth Seeds of a Great Opportunity Specific to You:

Begin with an idea. It's like a small seed. Then gather a measure of faith, and a deep desire for the seed to grow. Imagine the future of planting this seed. Does it align with your values and goals? Will you truly love it? Don't plant tomatoes if you dislike tomatoes. Only nurture what you believe you'll love.

Next, plant that seed, try it out in small ways. Nourish it for a time and observe if it sprouts. Ensure you've chosen fertile soil – even the hardiest seed fails in barren ground. Provide water and fertilizer – invest some resources – and watch what develops.

If the seed doesn't sprout and grow, you'll know early that it wasn't viable. If it sprouts, examine your response. Does it energize you? Illuminate your mind? Generate additional ideas and excitement? These are signs of a promising opportunity.

This next stage requires genuine humility – to see the plant honestly, not as you wish it to be. You must evaluate its potential to bear sufficient fruit to justify your investment. Mistakes here prove costly in resources, both material and emotional, forcing you to start anew with something different. Does it have enough scalability? Can it support you even in trying circumstances?

Faith remains essential throughout, but it grows stronger through your successes – even small ones. Try to gain deep understanding of what you've planted – like realizing a watermelon seed yields watermelon. Is watermelon what you really want? And keep watching your progress as you tend it properly.

Beware of neglecting proper cultivation steps. You know what's needed, but ignoring essentials like watering, weeding, fertilizing, ensuring adequate sunlight and pest protection will kill the tender plant, wasting your effort. You'll love most tasks, but some crucial ones you won't like at all. Do them anyway, or risk losing everything. Your growing plant doesn't care which work you enjoy.

Perfection isn't required – just enough consistency to meet your plant's needs. Faith remains necessary – there are no guarantees. But steady growth validates your faith, strengthening it as you see evidence of progress toward harvest.

As growth continues, monitor your feelings. Does your enthusiasm persist? Do you still feel energized and eager to work with it? Does the promise of future fruit sustain you through difficult tasks? Do you lose yourself in the work?

A strong seed continues growing. A weak one fades, growth stunts, the plant withers. Do you still love the work? Will it serve others? This proves most challenging.

At this stage, carefully distinguish between seed quality and cultivation. If the soil is poor or nourishment inadequate, the gardener must improve. If the seed proves weak despite proper care and good soil, it's time to uproot it and plant something new.

Faith, diligence, patience, and perseverance matter even with good seeds. But the harvest brings true delight, and the planting the seeds of the *right* opportunity nourishes you for life.

#

When Dan arrived home, he shared every detail of the meeting with Mandie. Her smile broadened when he described Blaine's emphasis on complete partnership and involvement. It grew even wider when Dan, grinning himself, mentioned his thoughts about "when a student is ready, a teacher will appear."

"He's a wise man," Mandie said. "And I don't think it's coincidence you met him just when you needed guidance for the next step."

Dan agreed. Then he handed her the laminated sheet, watching as her eyes widened while reading.

"It aligns perfectly with your dream!" Mandie exclaimed. "That's no coincidence. We should definitely follow this guidance. It makes perfect sense. Now we just need to help you discover what you truly love to do."

"How should we approach that?" Dan asked. "Should we make a list?"

Mandie paused thoughtfully, then said, "Not to dampen the mood, but you should see this before anyone asks about it."

She held up her phone screen pointing to a news headline. As their resident news enthusiast, she always devoured the daily news. Dan relied on her to keep him informed of important developments – yet another way they complemented each other.

The headline read: "Promising Start-up Goes Bust, Leaves Customers Holding Bag."

"Oh no," Dan said. His stomach churned as he read the article detailing his former company's bankruptcy and customers' complaints about unreturned deposits – deposits he had convinced them to make. His breath caught as he spotted his name listed among the ownership, just above mention of a launching fraud investigation.

"Just great!" Dan said.

Chapter Nine

The next morning, Dan sat at his makeshift office in the front room, phone pressed to his ear.

"I'm sorry, but I'm as much a victim as you." Dan struggled to keep his voice down, conscious of the kids elsewhere in the house... and Mandie in the kitchen. "I wish I could repay the money, but I was laid off. I wasn't really an owner – I just had a small stake in the company as part of my compensation. I've tried reaching the real owners, but they aren't returning my calls either. I'm doing everything I can to help. Really!"

Dan hung up and drew a deep breath, trying to steady himself. That made three calls from former customers today. Their predicament pained him deeply. *So much for serving others*, he thought bitterly. *More like hurting them.*

Turning to the stack of mail on his desk, he began sorting through envelopes. One caught his eye, and he tore it open, dread rising in his chest.

It was a notice of default. Unless they caught up on their mortgage payments, the company would foreclose on their home. They had thirty days to pay before the foreclosure notice would be posted and a sale scheduled. *This is not going to make Mandie happy.*

"The day just keeps getting better," Dan mumbled, stress mounting. *I can't afford the luxury of discovering what I love to do, much less figure out how it can serve others. I need to start earning money now!*

Taking another deep breath, Dan opened his planner and scanned the list of businesses where he'd submitted applications. The most productive thing right now would be securing a job. Any job!

He picked up the phone and reached the first Human Resources director.

"Hello, this is Anna."

"Hello," Dan said. "This is Dan Benjamin. I'm calling to follow up on my job application. I'd like to schedule an interview if possible. With my experience and ability, I believe I could be an asset to your company."

"Dan Benjamin, you say?" Paper shuffled in the background. "Oh yes, here it is." A pause stretched out. "I'm sorry, Mr. Benjamin, we're just not hiring right now. We'll keep your application on file and call you if something comes up." The line went dead.

Dan set down the phone. *That's odd*, he thought. *Her hesitation before the rejection.* An uncomfortable suspicion began to form. Dan pushed it aside and reached for the phone again. *Need to keep getting back on the horse. If I can bring Mandie some good news, it will soften the blow. Please, give me some good news*, he prayed as he dialed the next number...

Three more calls brought three more rejections. All were polite, claiming they weren't hiring. One asked if his previous employer was the company that had just declared bankruptcy. Dan's suspicions crystallized – he was being blacklisted because of his last position. No one would hire someone associated with that company, especially with fraud allegations in the picture.

So much for good news. Things just keep deteriorating. A fleeting thought of his dream surfaced – the tree, and the people lost in the canyon searching for their way. "Am I lost already?" Dan wondered aloud. "I didn't know I'd even moved that far along the path. I sure feel lost, though." Dan shook his head in wry frustration.

Chapter Ten

One week later.

"Mr. Shenk?" Dan peered into the classroom doorway. During Parent-Teacher conferences, he was covering Dan Jr.'s appointments while Mandie handled the other children's.

"Dan? Come in and have a seat."

Mr. Shenk taught chemistry and embodied every stereotype – thick glasses, plaid shirt, and polyester slacks hitched high. Even the white loafers, though Dan Jr. had confided that Mr. Shenk wore those purely for effect, a badge of Nerd Pride.

Dan entered and sat. Mr. Shenk settled into a chair opposite him, in front of the desk.

"Let's get straight to it," Mr. Shenk began. "First, call me Herman. The kids call me Mr. Shenk."

"Okay, Herman it is. And thank you, not just for teaching Dan Jr. chemistry, but for coaching his soccer team. I can't believe you're on track for another league title. What will it be if you win – seven in a row?"

Mr. Shenk was truly unique. Beyond being a universally enjoyed chemistry teacher, he volunteered to coach a city league soccer team despite having no children on the roster. In his ten years coaching, he'd claimed the league championship for the past six seasons, now possibly approaching seven. There was talk of promoting him to all-star coach for the regional traveling team.

"Don't mention it," Herman said. "By the way, you're my last appointment tonight, so there's no rush. Coaching Dan Jr. is a pleasure. Not only does he have talent, but he's got real drive. That's the critical element, you know. Drive.

"He's also an excellent chemistry student, near the top of the class. He'd probably lead it if he focused on chemistry more than soccer. Still, I won't complain. He's a major reason for our success this year. Again, it's his work ethic."

Pride swelled in Dan's chest. He knew Dan Jr. excelled at soccer – he'd scored twice in the last match. But hearing it confirmed by the coach felt special.

"Thanks," Dan replied. "It's his mother's influence. She's the one with talent in the family. Dan Jr. inherited it from her."

"What about the work ethic?"

"Well, I suppose I've set that example. Though sometimes I wonder if I'm teaching him the wrong things – I used to miss all his games because of work. I wish I'd spent more time with him there."

"We all wish we'd done things differently," Herman said. "The key is doing what you believe is right from this point forward. If you have regrets, then change course. Pretty simple."

"A chemistry professor, coach, and philosopher?"

"It's all chemistry, Dan. It's all chemistry."

"What?"

"You asked about the league titles? It's about chemistry. Want to understand life? It's about chemistry."

"Okay, tell me more," Dan said, suddenly intrigued. He sensed this conversation held something important.

"Well, I've covered what I needed to about Dan Jr. You know he's a good student, and you'll encourage his continued effort... So now we can discuss chemistry.

"Chemistry is all about reactions, interactions, and formulas. If you want a specific reaction or interaction, you follow a formula. Follow it correctly, and you'll get the desired result. It's a simple law, consistent and dependable.

"Many formulas for various reactions have already been identified. They give us what we seek every time. As a society, we've harnessed these to benefit our lives. Consider internal combustion, nuclear fission, and hopefully soon, nuclear fusion. There's electrolysis, insulin for diabetics, and countless other beneficial drugs. All rooted in chemistry.

"We're constantly exploring and developing new formulas to achieve desired reactions and interactions.

"But consider life itself – it's one grand formula. To obtain a certain outcome, we follow the formula. That's how we win the league title. We follow the formula."

Dan began to grasp the concept. "You've identified the formula for winning soccer matches?"

"I have," Herman grinned. "Discovered it six years ago. Took most of the previous four years, but I have it down now – with minor adjustments each season as conditions change and new players – new ingredients, you might say – join the team."

"You're serious," Dan said. "You've reduced it all to chemistry – to a formula."

"Seems to work, doesn't it?" Herman replied. "The scientific method relies on experimentation, and when you can replicate a successful experiment repeatedly, it approaches established fact."

"How did you accomplish it?" Dan asked, noting the parallel to his dream – the path he needed to identify and follow to reach his destination.

It amazed him that Dan Jr.'s chemistry teacher was essentially discussing the same concept Dan was trying to understand. The phrase *when a student is ready, a teacher will appear* surfaced in his mind. *Mandie will love hearing this has happened again.*

"To determine the formula, I studied what made soccer teams successful. Then I implemented those elements with the city league team. It took some experimentation and testing, but I developed the formula. The key is getting players to *buy in*. They make the team what it is.

"Each season begins with a deal. If they'll work harder than anyone else and follow my coaching, I guarantee them a successful season. More importantly, I promise they'll learn life lessons about achieving success.

"These kids push themselves in response. I structure the practices, drills, and strategy. They commit to the conditioning. I'm upfront about what's required, and they pledge to follow through. When they do, they see results from game one. It's self-correcting too – we analyze each game against the *formula* to identify where we've fallen short. The statistics provide proof."

"Dan Jr. mentioned your team tracks specific stats."

"It's integral to the formula. We've identified and monitor key components that drive our success. Then we focus strict attention on those components. That's what delivers results."

"This has been enlightening." Dan said, his mind racing with the implications for his own search. The key was first determining what he wanted to succeed at. He needed a target, a goal before he could find a formula or identify the *path*. Though he sensed he was on the right path, he needed greater specificity. And soon.

"Here, have a recipe for chocolate chip cookies. It's my favorite," Herman said, extending a 3x5 card with printed instructions. "A recipe is simply a formula for achieving a desired outcome. Include all ingredients and follow instructions correctly, and success is guaranteed! That's what I tell the kids."

Dan accepted the recipe, understanding perfectly what Mr. Shenk meant.

Chapter Eleven

Dan and Mandie lay in bed, their house dark and quiet, children asleep. The clock on Dan's nightstand read 11:42. They had just finished watching the news.

"How did your visit with Dan Jr.'s teacher go?" Mandie asked.

"Funny you should ask," Dan said, and shared his conversation with Mr. Shenk. "By the way, remind me to give you his recipe. It looks good."

"Wow," Mandie said. "Looks like you've had another one of *those* teachers. And it aligns perfectly with your dream. Being on the path to the tree is essentially the same as following a formula. Consider this another confirmation we're on the right track."

"For all the good it's doing us," Dan said. "I've been mulling it over since the meeting."

"That's why you've been so quiet," Mandie observed.

"The problem is," Dan continued as if she hadn't spoken, "I don't know how to apply it. I have these great principles to follow, but without a job to apply them to, what good are they? I feel like I'm loaded up for a journey I need to begin immediately, but I have no destination. All I can do is sit in the driveway and fret about going nowhere."

Mandie fell silent for a moment. "Maybe we're looking at this wrong. You're thinking you need to apply these principles to a job. What if you switched what you applied the principles to?"

"What do you mean?" Dan asked.

Another pause. "Well, what if, instead of thinking you should apply the *formula* or follow the *path* related to a job, what if you broadened your thinking and asked, *how do I use these principles to earn a living*?"

"Isn't that what I'm doing?" Dan asked.

"There's a difference," Mandie said. "I didn't mention a job. I said *earning a living*."

"Are you suggesting starting a business? We've already explored that, and the time it takes to start earning enough would be too late. We need money now. And while buying an established business might help, we have no down payment. Besides, our credit is probably ruined by now."

"No," Mandie said. "You're limiting your thinking again. I didn't mention starting a business. I said to use what you've learned to *earn a living*."

Dan pondered this. *What was Mandie trying to say*?

Mandie continued, "The problem is more basic than what job you have. The issue is that we need money to pay our bills. If we step back and think, okay, how can we get some money? Maybe that's what we should apply the principles to."

Dan considered this as silence filled the room. His mind shifted gears and something clicked.

"You're right! We can apply the principles to earning money. If we consider various formulas for making money, without limiting ourselves to just finding a job or starting a business, other possibilities emerge.

"I should register with the temp agency and take whatever work they offer while I'm job hunting."

"I've been thinking we should have a garage sale," Mandie said. "That could raise some money. And I've been looking into something else." Her voice wasn't tentative—it was the voice she used when she'd already done the analysis. "The school needs aides. The hours match the kids' schedule. It brings in income while keeping me available for them."

Dan was quiet for a moment. He'd sensed this was coming.

"This isn't me giving up on our plan," Mandie said. "This is me applying what I've been studying. We're an enterprise, Dan. Right now our enterprise needs a second revenue stream. That's not a failure—it's a strategy."

"I'm so sorry," Dan said, feeling as if the wind had been knocked from him. Mandie had felt strongly about staying home with their children. They had made their agreement standing over Dan Jr.'s crib fourteen years ago – Dan would provide for the family so Mandie could be there as the children grew up. Now that promise lay broken. Dan heard the logic. It was sound—her coursework talking, and she was right. But the weight of it still pressed on his chest. A year ago they'd said "It's time" on the couch and believed everything was about to change.

"I'll visit the temp agency first thing tomorrow and register for anything available. I'll also spread the word that I'm looking for work, even temporary positions."

"I know, Dan," Mandie snuggled closer. "I know. And don't worry. I know it's only temporary until things improve."

Dan's heart remained heavy.

After a stretch of silence, Mandie spoke again.

"Dan?"

"Yes?"

"I hate to bring this up, but have you heard anything about the mortgage?"

Dan drew a deep breath. "I have. I spoke with our representative about getting more time or pursuing one of those modifications we've heard about. He said we can't do the modification until I have a job. However, he mentioned they have a backlog on foreclosures in our area because of the plant closure, so our home isn't scheduled for advertisement and sale right now."

"What does that mean?" Mandie asked, tension evident in her body.

"From what he said, it appears we have several more months before a sale would occur. He estimated we have until year's end to get things in order."

"You're sure?" Mandie asked, relaxing slightly. "That's over six months?"

"I've read about people staying in their homes for up to a year. The rep said that could change, though, and couldn't make any guarantees.

"At minimum, we'd have three months' notice because that's the required advertising period for a foreclosure sale."

"That's somewhat relieving," Mandie said, falling silent again. Dan sensed she had more to say.

"What is it?" he finally asked.

"Please don't be angry," she said. "I enrolled the kids in free school lunch. And... I applied for food stamps. I figured we needed to conserve money wherever possible. I know how much pressure you're under, and I know you're doing everything you can..."

Dan pulled Mandie closer, as much for his own comfort as hers. This time he couldn't hold back the tears. The tears came not from shame but from the sheer weight of how hard they'd been trying and how far they still had to go. "I'm sorry you had to make that call without me."

"I'm so sorry," was all he could manage as tears streamed down his face.

"I know it's temporary. Just think of all the signs we've received – your dream, and the teachers appearing just when needed, all confirming the dream's message. I know things will improve. We just have to hold on and get through this." Mandie hugged Dan fiercely. "I love you, Dan Benjamin, and we will overcome this!"

Chapter Twelve

The next morning, Dan had signed up with two temp agencies in town. The first immediately placed him, and for three days he'd had steady work. Though it paid just above minimum wage – basic labor loading and unloading trucks – it was income.

Simply doing something had started to lift his spirits. Today's assignment had been just a half day, and now that it was complete, Dan was home preparing to follow up on his submitted applications. *May as well do some phone work*, he thought.

He was reaching for the phone when it rang.

"Hello?"

"Hello. Is this Dan?"

"Yes."

"Dan, I don't know if you remember me. This is Frank Truesome with Wild Boar Ventures."

"Yes, I remember. How are you, Frank?"

"Well, not so good. Remember that investment we placed with your company?"

"Yes." Dan tensed. This was another one of *those* calls.

"Well, the amount we provided, based on promises about your product being nearly ready, has severely hurt our cash flow. We know your company has declared bankruptcy, but we need that money now. I'm calling to see if you can help recover our investment."

"I'm sorry, Frank," Dan said. "According to the owners, the money is gone, and they've filed to dissolve the company."

Silence stretched across the line. When Frank finally spoke, his voice was taut with tension.

"Then I'm afraid we'll have to proceed with our suit."

Dan gripped the phone, his breath catching. He sensed something terrible approaching.

"On our attorney's advice, we're filing suit against your company and the owners individually. The company registration shows you as an owner. Since I know you, I wanted to give you one last chance to make this right before proceeding. If you can't help me, then I guess all I can say is, I'll see you in court."

The line went dead.

Dan drew a deep breath, but it brought no relief. A lawsuit was the last thing he needed. How much would an attorney cost? What did that matter? They couldn't afford one anyway. Maybe the company had insurance to help. Dan knew he should have insisted on greater involvement in management, now realizing ownership brought as much liability as benefit.

What would Mandie think? He considered keeping it from her to protect her and the kids, then remembered his promise to involve her in everything. Better she hear it from him than discover it later.

The tension in his chest intensified until he worried about a heart attack. He needed to calm down and think. Dan went to the kitchen for aspirin, having heard it helped during heart attacks. What were the symptoms? He had to get himself under control.

He retreated to the garage, switched on the light, and settled at his workbench. He'd work on figurines. Christmas approached, and he could productively create gifts for the neighbors. Working with the wire always calmed him, helped him think. Dan picked up the soldering iron and began shaping the wire...

#

"Dad? You in here?" Dan Jr. walked into the garage and stood beside him.

"You're home already?" Dan glanced at the clock and realized he'd worked straight through two hours. He'd completed nine figurines in that time – one every fifteen minutes.

"Just got back from school," Dan Jr. said, examining the completed figurines. "These are really cool. Could you make one for Mr. Shenk? Like a chemistry teacher?"

"I suppose I could," Dan said.

"Here," Dan Jr. said, extending a twenty-dollar bill.

"What's this?"

"It's payment for Mr. Shenk's . . . thingy. What do you call them?"

"They're figurines," Dan said. "And where did you get twenty dollars?"

"Mr. Shenk gave it to me. I took my... figurine to school to show my friends. Mr. Shenk saw it and asked if you could make him one. Maybe he'd prefer a soccer player instead of a chemistry teacher. I'll have to ask him."

"What about the twenty dollars?" Dan prompted.

"Oh yeah. Mr. Shenk asked how much you charged. I didn't know, so I said twenty dollars. He pulled out his wallet right there. He said he'd pay more if needed."

Dan stared at the money.

"So, will you do it? Or should I charge more?" Dan Jr. asked.

Dan snapped out of his daze. "Give Mr. Shenk his money back," he said, smiling to soften the instruction. "Tell him that teaching and coaching you is payment enough. And tell him he'll get both a chemistry teacher *and* a soccer player."

"Wow Dad! He'll love that!"

"It's the least I can do." Dan felt his burden lighten slightly. Not much, but creating something others appreciated helped ease his mind.

Chapter Thirteen

Mid-July arrived. Dan remained jobless, understanding why. The newspapers constantly reported possible criminal activities at his previous company, deterring any decent employer from considering him.

Jobs existed, yes, but none that could support their needs. Mandie had secured work as a school aide, with hours matching the children's schedule. Her income covered utilities, clothing, and car payments. His temporary work had allowed some mortgage payments, but not enough to bring it current. They'd surrendered one car, unable to maintain payments. Their credit was beyond repair, eliminating any prospect of loans.

The legal action from his previous employment loomed overhead, with potential criminal charges threatening. He wondered how it might affect him, if he'd be named. Given his luck lately, probably.

A recent letter from an attorney had arrived, alleging various improprieties and demanding repayment with interest and penalties. His copy matched the original sent to the former owners. As a partial owner, he'd been included. Dan knew he needed his own attorney – he couldn't trust his former bosses to protect his interests. They obviously had problems of their own. His attempts to contact them had proved as futile as everyone else's.

Good attorneys cost money – money he didn't have. His ship was sinking, and Dan felt like he was bailing desperately to stay afloat.

Now he stood at the edge of City Common, a sprawling park hosting community events. Across the broad lawn, vendors erected tent-booths for tomorrow's Summer Festival. The two-week celebration would feature crafts and entertainment. Through one of his temp agencies, Dan had secured a position as a temporary salesman, his sales experience qualifying him despite his recent troubles.

The job paid above minimum wage and offered sales performance bonuses. Though not ideal, it beat loading trucks. He was aging out of such labor-intensive work anyway.

Dan consulted the paper in his hand and walked down a row of booths until he reached #37.

Inside the canvas booth, a man unpacked boxes onto display tables.

"Hello?" Dan called.

The man looked up. He wore denim jeans and a black and brown plaid flannel shirt. His brown curly hair matched his well-trimmed beard. *He must be roasting*, Dan thought, noting the 85-degree heat of the California desert.

"Hello." The man extended his hand. "I'm Paul Rosenthal. You must be Dan Benjamin?"

"I am. Pleased to meet you," Dan said. "Here, this is for you. A small thank you for the two-week opportunity." Dan presented one of his figurines, shaped like a shopkeeper behind a cash register and table.

"You made this?" Paul studied it closely. "It's excellent. Captures a certain spirit despite its simple wire construction. I like it. Do you have more?"

"Well..." Dan hesitated, caught off guard. "I'm not trying to sell anything. I'm just here for the sales position."

"Of course, and I'm glad to have you. But part of sales is having something to sell. If you have more of these, I'll display them in the booth and we'll split the profits. What do you say?"

"Sure!" Dan said.

"This really is good," Paul continued examining the figurine. "It captures retail's essence while remaining playful. These could sell well. Do you have different types? I can envision a whole series."

"I've done several. I create them as needed. It's just a hobby – something I do to relax. I lose track of time working on them in my garage."

"That's the best kind of work. Happens to me too. Notice I don't wear a watch."

Dan looked. He didn't.

"Don't need one," Paul continued. "Don't care what time it is. I love the work and the people I meet. I eat when hungry, rest when tired, and otherwise focus on what I love.

"And I mean it about your figurines. You might have something here. Can you bring five for tomorrow morning? Let's see, you could do a fisherman, a businessman, a cowboy and...?"

"I've done a soccer player and a teacher," Dan interjected. "I'll create the others tonight. It only takes about twenty minutes each once I've visualized the concept."

"Perfect!" Paul exclaimed. "We'll display them and see how they perform. Any price in mind?"

"Someone offered twenty dollars and said they'd pay more."

"How about $19.99? It's a good price point that matches my other merchandise. What's your material cost? Can't be much."

"About a dollar per piece. I haven't calculated my time."

"No way! That's an incredible margin. You might have a winner here. We'll split the sales and you'll still see great profit. Does that work?"

"Sure." Dan tried to process what was happening. Beyond his regular earnings, he could profit from his creations. Then it struck him – perhaps he'd just met another of his *teachers*.

"Come on in," Paul said. "Help me set up and we'll reserve space for your pieces. I try new products every year, and if these sell well, I might want to keep ordering for my other shows. I maintain a website too. Any objections to online listings? Of course, it depends on sales and pricing."

"Sure." Dan contained his excitement.

He followed Paul into the booth, listening as Paul offered directions in an almost continuous stream. Dan worked and listened. And listened. And listened.

Paul was essentially a gypsy. He couldn't bear being indoors and loved meeting people. His first office job had driven him crazy, so he'd become a door-to-door salesperson, buying cheap items to resell at a profit. That led to his current success – several stores throughout northern California. He spent most of his time traveling to shows, testing new products and meeting people.

He took February through April off, then returned to the road. The business provided well – he owned his store properties and other investments. His wife urged retirement since they didn't need the money. Paul preferred traveling. He had too many friends to keep up with. Besides, what could he enjoy more?

Clearly, Paul loved his work and, in his unique way, served others. Dan thought of the Fluffy Bunny king and Mr. Shenk. All three had found their own success. More importantly, they seemed happy, fulfilled, excited about life. Dan craved that for himself and wanted to absorb every lesson possible.

Paul explained merchandising techniques as they worked, discussing how and why items should be displayed certain ways. He covered pricing, sales techniques, and cost analysis. Then he delved into location strategy, product mix, and inventory control.

Dan's questions sparked detailed explanations covering aspects he hadn't considered. It felt like a master class in retail business, peppered with entertaining stories about Paul's failures and friendships along the way.

An idea began forming in Dan's mind, and he wanted to learn everything possible. He sensed movement along the path toward his Tree, making the Ultimate Investment. The memory of that sublime fruit's taste seemed to return. He couldn't wait to share with Mandie, then get back to his garage and work.

Chapter Fourteen

As Dan pulled up to his house, he noticed an unfamiliar black SUV parked on the street. Something about it felt ominous. He parked in the garage and entered through the kitchen door into the living room, where Mandie sat with two men in dark suits who rose as he entered.

"Dan," Mandie said, "This is Agent Sperling and Agent Druthers. They're from the FBI and they want to talk with you."

Dan shook their hands and gestured for them to sit. He and Mandie took chairs facing the couch.

"What can I do for you?" Dan asked, though he already knew. That knowledge did nothing to ease the dread spreading through his chest.

"Mr. Benjamin," Agent Sperling said. "We'd like to ask you some questions regarding your previous employment with Contra Pro, Inc."

#

The interview lasted an hour, with Dan answering every question completely honestly. He had nothing to hide and wanted no appearance of concealment. Neither agent revealed whether they believed him, responding only with nods as Agent Druthers took notes on a small pad from his jacket pocket. Though cordial and friendly, they remained direct. Then they left.

"Whew, I'm glad that's over," Mandie said. "Before you ask, the kids are at the neighbors. I didn't want them coming in and out. It'll be difficult enough when neighborhood gossip starts."

Dan nodded, only half-listening. He was reviewing the questions they'd asked, sensing they were fishing to determine if his involvement ran deeper than claimed. He mentally retraced his answers – complete, honest, and direct. Hopefully, they couldn't misconstrue anything. Truth was the best defense, wasn't it?

#

At dinner that evening, Dan shared his experience with Paul and the potential for selling figurines. He asked the kids for design ideas. Their suggestions leaned toward sports, though Melissa insisted on including a Mom figurine – "because moms are the hardest workers and nobody makes figurines of them."

Dan made a list and promised to test several designs. The kids proposed a contest to determine the best idea, with the winner receiving an unshared bag of Oreos.

After the children went to bed, Dan and Mandie moved to the garage where he could work on figurines for tomorrow's fair. As Dan gathered tools and cut wire lengths, Mandie settled into a metal folding chair beside the workbench.

"Are you thinking what I'm thinking?" Mandie asked.

"Don't know," Dan answered, continuing his work. The process felt almost automatic now. "What are you thinking?"

"I think you know," Mandie teased. "I think you're considering whether this might be a *seed* you could nurture into a business."

Dan turned and smiled at his wife.

"At minimum, it's a perfect way to *plant the seed*, test the concept, and earn while doing it. Looking at Blaine's sheet, this seems to fit."

They reviewed the criteria together, finding the opportunity aligned well so far.

"And you've found another *teacher*," Mandie observed.

"Indeed. The way he naturally shared his business knowledge while we worked was incredible. It feels meant to be." Dan paused thoughtfully. "I feel like I'm walking a path I was destined to find."

Mandie smiled, tears glistening. "I feel it too, but we need to proceed cautiously. We have bills to handle."

"Agreed. This is just a test. If it shows promise, we can expand. I know our priority is meeting our obligations."

They worked in comfortable silence for a moment.

"You know," Dan said, breaking the quiet, "my teachers share common traits. Each loves their work. Each serves others uniquely. And each follows an unconventional path. None took what I'd consider an ordinary route."

"That's true," Mandie agreed. "I suspect most people who truly love their work and serve others don't concern themselves with convention."

"Exactly what Blaine said! Each teacher created their own path and made it work," Dan mused. "They discovered what they loved and found ways to earn from it."

"They've solved the equation," Mandie said, thinking of Mr. Shenk. "They've followed the recipe. They've made the Ultimate Investment."

"Paul's definitely sharing his recipe with me," Dan said.

"Indeed," Mandie said. "Pay close attention. We can't afford to miss any ingredients."

Chapter Fifteen

Over the next two weeks, Dan split his time between the festival during the day and creating figurines at night. The first day, all five figurines sold before noon. Paul requested double for the next day, and they strategized about which designs to try. The second day's inventory also sold out, with customers requesting additional varieties.

After consulting Mandie, Dan asked Paul to mentor him in exploring whether the figurines could provide not just a business, but a *living*.

Paul enthusiastically agreed. While he couldn't guarantee the figurines would sustain them, he offered to help investigate the possibility.

Each evening after closing the booth, they gathered at the local Denny's near the Commons. Paul shared his expertise while Mandie joined them with her folder and calculator, ready to run the numbers.

Their first task, sketched on a napkin, was calculating potential earnings. Using the well-received price point of $19.99 and $1.00 cost per unit, they had an $18.99 margin per piece.

The key question was whether Dan could produce and sell enough figurines to support his family. If not, he'd need help, which would increase costs.

Dan could create three figurines per hour – four with simpler, familiar designs – generating potential gross income of $65-70 hourly. Business expenses would come from that.

Paul outlined Dan's options: retail or wholesale. As a retailer, he'd earn $18.99 per figurine but face costs for shelf space, employees, location, and set hours. As a wholesaler, he'd split his margin with retailers like Paul, earning $9.99 per piece. This route meant lower expenses, flexible hours, and no location concerns, plus potential for greater volume through multiple outlets.

Paul walked them through the retail and wholesale models while Mandie tracked the figures in her notebook, cross-referencing against their monthly expenses. She was the one who identified the break-even point—twenty-five figurines a day at retail would cover expenses and help them catch up on bills by Christmas.

Given they were already selling ten daily with minimal display at the festival, twenty-five seemed achievable with proper presentation.

Dan saw potential for earning a modest but sufficient living. The key was establishing an effective retail location.

Paul's expertise proved invaluable as he suggested focusing on the Christmas season with a temporary mall booth. Dan had learned booth operations working with Paul and felt ready. They decided to follow Paul's *recipe* and proceed!

The festival's two weeks yielded $3,500 from wages, bonuses, and figurine sales, averaging ten pieces daily. Paul agreed to carry the figurines in his stores, traveling booths, and website, maintaining the $19.99 price point. Dan would fulfill orders as received.

Dan planned to research and establish his top fifteen designs before building inventory.

On the festival's final afternoon, Mandie helped Dan and Paul pack up. Their goodbye felt like parting with family. Dan and Mandie both hugged Paul farewell.

"Not farewell," Paul said, grinning broadly. "Until the next order – which will be soon!"

After Paul's van disappeared, Dan turned to Mandie. "Remember the path... the dream?"

"I feel it too," Mandie said. "I believe this is going to work."

#

"It sure didn't take long to come back down to earth," Dan said to Mandie as they sat on the couch. It was mid-afternoon, two days after the summer festival ended. Heat permeated the house – they kept the cooler at a higher temperature setting to conserve on utilities. The kids had found refuge at a neighbor's pool, trying to stay cool.

After meeting with Paul and developing their plan – their *path* – they'd both felt hope blossoming, seeing light at the end of the tunnel. Now that hope dimmed, the light fading.

"The lawyer needs a three-thousand-dollar retainer. I convinced him to accept two thousand now with the remaining thousand by month's end."

"Where will that come from?" Mandie asked.

"I'll look for temp work to keep money flowing. I'll also approach boutiques about carrying the figurines. Something will emerge. Paul's bound to place an order soon. Maybe it'll be large enough to cover it."

"Maybe," she said flatly. "We're still far behind on house payments too. We haven't made a full payment in three months. Any word on the auction date?"

"The mortgage company rep says we're not scheduled until after New Year's."

"That gives us some breathing room, at least," Mandie said. "We'll manage utilities and the remaining car payment. Not much else. What about materials for the figurines? What if we can't complete orders?"

Dan recognized the signs of Mandie beginning to unravel. These moments were rare but intense. The pressure had worn her down more than she'd revealed. He pulled her into an embrace, holding her close. She began to shudder, then deep sobs wracked her small frame. Though she fought to contain them, the emotions wouldn't be denied.

"It's okay," Dan whispered, stroking her hair.

"Why can't things work out for us? Why can't life ease up just a little?"

"I wish I knew," Dan answered, pressing his lips to the top of her head, ashamed of the tears tracking down his own cheeks.

Chapter Sixteen

"We're going to survive the month!" Dan announced two days later, entering the kitchen and settling at the dining table. Mandie set aside her dishcloth, kissed him, and joined him.

"I'm sorry again about my breakdown. I should be stronger. Thank you for holding steady."

Dan nodded. "You just needed to release some pressure. Besides, you embody strength. And truth be told, it was your turn. I already had mine."

Mandie laughed. "I assume Paul's order came through? We can pay the attorney and get materials?"

"You are correct, lovely lady."

Dan had negotiated with Paul for a figurine order with immediate payment – at a discount for the cash. Paul readily agreed, recognizing both the good deal and their urgent need.

Paul had remarked that necessity truly was the mother of invention. Dan agreed, finally understanding the old saying's meaning. He hoped they'd endure the stress long enough to escape living hand-to-mouth, perpetually behind. The strain affected everyone – even the kids, though Mandie largely shielded them.

"What's next?" Mandie asked.

"Here's the plan: I'll visit professionals to get their opinions on figurines representing their fields. I'll also start investigating mall spaces for Christmas. I don't want to delay too long."

"But it's only August," Mandie said.

"I'll keep taking temporary work and searching for permanent positions while creating more figurines. The Christmas selling season starts in November. It's a ways off, with minimal income. With what I'm doing – investing all my Ultimate Investment – something positive must emerge. We're due."

Mandie nodded silently. Dan could tell she still felt guilty about her recent breakdown. "It will happen!" she finally declared.

"I've been wondering about our position on the path to the Tree," Dan said. "Where do you think we are? Are we nearing the tree?"

"I certainly hope so," Mandie said. "Funny, I pondered that this morning while you were out. Remember in your dream, that low point where you couldn't see the tree ahead or your past progress? When all you could do was trust and keep moving? I think that's our current spot."

"I think you're right," Dan said after careful consideration. "I'm hoping... really hoping things improve. We *need* them to work out somehow."

"Then we must have faith," Mandie said. "And keep walking the path." She glanced toward the kitchen, where the wooden plaque on the refrigerator caught the afternoon light. Seven words. Some days they felt like a lifeline. Other days—days like this—they felt like a prayer that hadn't been answered yet. But Elizabeth had known what she was talking about. She'd lost a sister, lost a husband, built a business from nothing, and kept going. If she could walk on rough ground and not stop, so could they.

Chapter Seventeen

Dan pursued the plan with determination. He secured temporary work to maintain cash flow while fulfilling growing orders from Paul, who stocked his stores and sold figurines at shows. He met countless friends and associates, showing his creations. Most responded enthusiastically, offering valuable suggestions. Some purchased pieces as gifts. Several local boutiques invited him to display his work, generating steady sales. He told everyone to watch for his Christmas mall booth. Every free moment went to crafting his top fifteen designs, limited only by time and resources.

The hours spent creating figurines refreshed him like cool water. Despite working late while exhausted, he found renewal in the craft. Several hours would pass before Mandie appeared to gently scold him about the late hour.

Dan enjoyed working independently, even without immediate financial reward. He prayed the money would follow because he truly loved the work – really loved it. He occasionally recalled the fruit's sublime taste, sensing hints of that satisfaction now and then.

His inventory grew alongside his hope. Each figurine bore his mark: a small crease on the bottom of the right foot, symbolizing his journey on the *path*. This signature reminded him to maintain his highest standards, quality he'd always take pride in.

\#

While Dan built his inventory, Mandie carried her own quiet thread.

On a Saturday morning in late August, she drove to Elizabeth's house. She hadn't told Dan—not because it was a secret, but because it was hers. A conversation she needed to have with someone who understood what it meant to build something from nothing.

Michael opened the door. He looked better than the last time she'd seen him—rested, more settled, though the house behind him still had the careful quiet of a place being tended.

"Mandie." He smiled warmly. "I was hoping you'd come back. Coffee?"

They sat in Elizabeth's library, in the wingback chairs, with the cane still leaning by the door. Mandie held her coffee and told Michael everything—Contra Pro's collapse, the temp work, the figurines, the mounting bills, the foreclosure threat. She told him about her school aide job and her coursework. She told him things she hadn't told Dan, because Dan was carrying enough and she didn't want to add her fear to his.

Michael listened the way his mother had listened—carefully, without hurry.

When she finished, he was quiet for a moment. Then he said, "You know, Mom nearly lost her business twice."

Mandie looked up. "Elizabeth?"

"Twice. The first time was three years in. She'd expanded too fast—hired too many people, took on too much overhead. Dad bailed her out with a loan from his own savings. She paid back every cent, but she said that failure taught her more than any success she'd ever had. The second time was after Dad died. She nearly shut the company down out of grief. She couldn't see the point without him."

"What kept her going?"

"Us. Me and my sister. And the women who worked for her—the seamstresses, the designers. She said she realized her time wasn't just hers anymore. Other people were counting on how she invested it. So she kept going." He paused. "Sound familiar?"

Mandie set her coffee down. It did sound familiar. It sounded exactly like her kitchen table, her spreadsheets, her coursework at midnight.

"Michael, I don't know exactly where it's leading yet. But I keep thinking about your mother—how she started with nothing and built something real. I think about that a lot."

Michael studied her for a moment—the same unhurried look his mother used to give. Then he stood.

"Wait here."

He disappeared into the back of the house and returned with a small leather-bound notebook, its cover worn smooth from years of handling.

"Mom kept this during the early years of the business. It's not a diary exactly—more like notes to herself. Lessons she was learning, mistakes she didn't want to repeat, ideas she was testing." He held it out. "I think she'd want you to have it."

Mandie took the notebook between her hands. The leather was soft, and when she opened it, she recognized Elizabeth's handwriting immediately—the same careful letters from the clues in the library, from the final letter Dan had read aloud on the couch. But these notes were younger, bolder—the writing of a woman who was still figuring things out, still making mistakes, still getting back up.

"Are you sure?" Mandie asked.

"She gave you the silk because you had the eyes," Michael said. "I'm giving you this because you have the mind. She would have loved watching you work through those business courses, Mandie. She would have seen herself in you."

Mandie held the notebook against her chest and didn't trust herself to speak for a long moment.

"Thank you, Michael."

"Come back anytime. The coffee's always on."

She drove home with the notebook on the passenger seat beside her, the August sun warm through the windshield. That evening, after the kids were in bed, she opened it at the kitchen table and began to read. Elizabeth's voice was there in every line—practical, honest, occasionally frustrated, always determined. On the third page, underlined twice, Mandie found a sentence that stopped her:

"The business will fail as many times as it needs to before it succeeds. My job is to outlast the failures."

Mandie closed the notebook, held it for a moment, then set it beside her manila folder. Two women's notes, fifty years apart, both learning the same lessons.

#

Then came the obstacle. Among the three regional malls and one smaller quasi-mall in his area, Dan approached the larger venues first about Christmas season booth space. Each appreciated his products and predicted success. Then came the rental terms.

The lowest price demanded $3,000 upfront by October 1st, covering rent, utilities, marketing, and bond. Another $3,000 payment would be due December 1st. The figures made his head spin. Their excess funds had gone to bills and legal fees. He couldn't manage those amounts.

He attempted negotiation. None would budge. They offered waitlist spots but expressed doubt without proper capital.

Discouraged, he tried the final location, considered quasi-mall status for its mixed indoor-outdoor design. Once innovative, the twenty-year-old concept had devolved into a run-down, half-empty shopping center.

Dan observed the minimal foot traffic from the central court. The prospects seemed dim. Even with space here, would sufficient customers appear?

The manager proved more accommodating. A kiosk space required only a $1,000 deposit by October 1st, covering utilities, marketing, and bond throughout the lease. Rent would be 8% of net sales, paid weekly.

She found his figurines delightful and predicted strong sales.

The rent structure relieved Dan. Lower traffic wouldn't threaten fixed costs – he'd only owe a percentage of actual sales.

His kiosk would occupy a prime spot near the central court, where holiday entertainment featuring school groups, choruses, and bands attracted crowds. The manager emphasized how these performances boosted foot traffic.

Dan fervently hoped so – he was counting on it. He and Mandie had envisioned a successful holiday season bringing their bills current – including mortgage payments. Of course, that assumed placement in a busier, upscale mall.

Once again, everything balanced on a knife's edge.

Chapter Eighteen

October 1st arrived swiftly, and they barely scraped together the thousand dollars needed for the Christmas kiosk deposit. Dan approached Paul again, who graciously arranged another cash sale – with a corresponding discount on the products. Dan's substantial inventory made the discount acceptable. The immediate cash was crucial. Sales through other outlets remained modest but steady. People appreciated his work, which brought satisfaction, but limited distribution meant minimal earnings. Besides, he was reserving inventory for the Christmas season when he wouldn't share profits.

The lawsuit had intensified. Attorneys exchanged endless paperwork, with Dan's counsel consistently denying wrongdoing. Depositions loomed. Legal fees had consumed another three thousand dollars, leaving them with precisely zero dollars on November 1st – the day he began at the quasi-mall.

#

Dan arrived early to set up his kiosk. Excitement filled the air as other vendors prepared their spaces. A balloon vendor, crystal glass sculptor, and stuffed animal kiosk surrounded the common area with him. Applying Paul's lessons, he arranged his merchandise to maximize customer appeal and encourage browsing. By 10:00 AM, he stood ready for sales.

By 11:30, he questioned everything. He'd counted eleven people passing his kiosk. Two had paused to comment on his interesting figurines before moving on. No sales. Dan wondered if he'd miscalculated something in his *equation* or missed an ingredient in his *recipe*.

Paul had emphasized location as crucial for retail success. Dan knew his spot was subpar, but it was all he could afford. Had that compromise proven fatal? He recalled the lost, frustrated people in his dream who had strayed from the path. His own frustration mounted.

Nothing to do now but see it through.

At noon, Mandie arrived with lunch. She surveyed the space, then turned to Dan. "Where are all the people?"

"I was about to ask you," Dan said. "Have they blocked the entrances? I haven't sold a thing."

"The entrance I used was open," Mandie replied, belatedly catching his irony.

She watched the kiosk while Dan visited the restroom. They talked as he ate.

"Maybe it's just Tuesday," Mandie suggested.

"Yeah, probably," Dan agreed.

Neither believed it. They fell silent, each afraid to voice their fear that this might have been a mistake.

Finally, Mandie spoke. "Well, I need to get back to school. Good luck. I'm sure things will pick up when the performances start."

"I'm sure they will," Dan said, watching her leave. He wished he could offer reassurance, but he needed some himself.

#

Activity increased slightly later in the day. After school, teenagers began appearing. Around 6:00 PM, Mandie brought dinner.

"Any improvement?" she asked.

"Some," Dan said. "One sale."

"That's good," Mandie agreed.

Dan took his bathroom break and quickly ate upon returning. Their conversation remained sparse.

"Think you can maintain the schedule?" Mandie asked.

They'd decided against hiring help. Dan would work all shifts to maximize their income. They needed every penny. Mandie would bring meals and cover brief bathroom breaks.

Holiday hours would run 9:00 AM to 10:00 PM daily starting after Thanksgiving. Current hours were 10:00 AM to 9:00 PM Monday through Saturday, with shorter Sunday hours of 11:00 AM to 5:00 PM.

"If it stays this quiet, it'll be a piece of cake," Dan said. He immediately regretted the words when he caught Mandie's worried expression.

"I'm sure it'll improve," he added quickly. "Like you said, it's Tuesday and still early."

"Right," Mandie agreed, unconvincingly.

Chapter Nineteen

"Oh, hey, Dear," Dan said, surprised. "Is it lunch already?"

"You sound cheerful," Mandie noted, setting the soft-sided lunch cooler inside the kiosk. "I brought the young ones to remind them they still have a father."

"Hi Dad," Dan Jr. said, waving while scanning the mall like his siblings. "Can I visit the arcade?"

"Me too," the others chorused.

"Briefly," Mandie said. "Danny, you're in charge. Watch your brother and sister."

"Here," Dan said, retrieving change from the cash box. "You need working capital for that venture."

"Thanks Dad!" Dan Jr. said.

"Make sure you share," Dan called after their retreating forms.

Dan laughed and embraced Mandie.

"Good to see you smiling," she said. "What's the occasion?"

"It's Saturday and people are finally appearing. Five sales this morning."

"That's wonderful!"

"Plus, I've been talking with a veteran vendor. See that stuffed animal kiosk? He's been here five years, supplementing his retirement. According to him, traffic builds gradually. Saturdays –

like today – stay fairly busy until Thanksgiving. Then it becomes a madhouse through season's end."

"That's encouraging." Mandie agreed.

Dan opened his lunch container. "Though sales are still modest, I expect improvement. Hopefully enough to meet our needs. Jerome – that's who I mentioned – knows his numbers. I've been learning from his experience."

"What does he think of your figurines?" Mandie asked.

"He likes them. Says they're perfect for kiosk business. He suggested creating my own website, and to hand out cards with the web address. Says it helps off-season sales. That's his approach."

"Sounds promising." Mandie said.

"I'll bring the laptop to work on the site during slow periods. Jerome offered to show me setup for about twenty-five dollars. I'll need the digital camera and a black sheet for product photography."

"We're entering the next business phase," Mandie observed. "Will Paul mind? He carries your work on his site."

"Already checked," Dan said, holding up his phone. "He loves the idea. Plus, he's placed another large order. The figurines are succeeding in all his outlets, including online. He says my website won't compete because he draws different traffic."

"The engine's gathering steam," Mandie said, visibly relieved.

"Can you watch the shop while I take a break?"

Mandie nodded with a genuine smile.

#

His first Saturday ended with four additional sales. Though below their target, momentum was building. He hoped average sales would reach the level needed to save their house. Time was running short, and they had no backup plan. All their energy focused on the kiosk.

Though he hadn't developed alternatives, he suspected Mandie was considering them privately, staying silent to maintain his focus. That would be typical of her.

Stress crept back as he bent to store inventory beneath the locked kiosk shelves before closing.

He straightened to find an older gentleman in a business suit waiting patiently.

"Hello," Dan said. "I've packed away the figurines, but if you're looking for something specific, I can retrieve it."

The man stood about six-foot-two, slender, wearing a gray pinstripe three-piece suit. His thinning gray hair and deep tan projected a somewhat affected dignity that almost made Dan smile.

"I'd like to look at your businessman and businesswoman figurines. My wife saw them earlier and recommended them to me. I want to give them as gifts to my managers. There's twelve of them. Do you have that in stock? Or can I place and order and have my secretary pick them up?"

"I'd be happy to take your order . . ." It was enough to push back the stress and allow a bit of hope to peek through.

Chapter Twenty

It happened on a Thursday afternoon, an hour before closing. Dan was restocking the kiosk shelves when a man in a charcoal sport coat approached with the easy confidence of someone who belonged everywhere he went.

"These are yours?" The man picked up a figurine—the soccer player—and turned it slowly in his fingers. "Exceptional work. Truly. The detail is remarkable."

"Thank you," Dan said. "Each one's handmade. Can I help you find something?"

The man set the figurine down and extended his hand. "Raymond Chandler. I represent specialty products to gift shops and boutiques across the region. Ten stores currently, with plans to expand." He smiled. "I've been watching your kiosk for a few days. Your product is something my retailers are looking for."

Dan felt a spark of excitement. Ten stores. That kind of distribution could change everything.

Raymond laid out his pitch with practiced ease. He could place Dan's figurines in ten stores by Thanksgiving. He'd handle all the retail relationships, displays, and shelf placement. Dan would just need to supply inventory and pay fifteen hundred dollars upfront for display materials and shelf-space deposits—standard practice, Raymond assured him. He projected eight thousand dollars in Christmas season orders, conservatively.

"I need an answer quickly," Raymond said. "Three weeks to Thanksgiving. If we're not on shelves by then, we miss the season entirely."

"What stores are you in?" Dan asked.

"That's confidential. I wouldn't want you to go around me."

"Oh, that makes sense. How about references? Do you have a contract I can review?

"I don't provide references for the same reason. They'd all be with the stores I represent. As for contracts, a simple verbal agreement has always sufficed me in the past with those who have taken advantage of the opportunity I offered. No one has ever complained—especially after I've delivered their checks."

Dan took Raymond's card. "Let me talk it over with my wife. I'll call you tomorrow."

Raymond's smile tightened almost imperceptibly. "Don't wait too long. Opportunities like this don't come around twice."

That night in bed, Dan told Mandie everything. He could hear the excitement in his own voice and tried to temper it, but the numbers were intoxicating—eight thousand dollars could make the difference between saving and losing the house.

Mandie listened without interrupting. When he finished, she was quiet for a long moment.

"What do we know about him?" she asked.

"He gave me his card. Raymond Chandler, specialty product representation."

"Can we check references? Talk to his other clients?"

Dan related his conversation about references and contracts.

Mandie was quiet again. Dan could feel her thinking in the dark.

"Dan. No references. Cash upfront. Pressure to decide immediately. No contracts—he told you that, right?"

"He said if trust fails, either party can walk away with no remaining obligation."

"That's not how legitimate business works." Her voice was steady—the voice of a woman who had been studying business management for over a year. "Every real distributor Paul introduced us to wanted invoices, purchase orders, documentation. Paul insisted on it. This man wants cash and a handshake."

Dan felt the excitement draining out of him, replaced by something heavier. She was right. He'd known she was right even as he was telling her, but the numbers had been so good, and they were so desperate.

"Remember what Elizabeth taught us," Mandie said softly. "She wouldn't give you the easy answer because she knew what easy answers do to people. This man is offering us an easy answer, Dan. Eight thousand dollars, just like that. *When has anything worth having come to us just like that?*"

The bedroom was quiet. Dan stared at the ceiling.

"You're right," he said. "I'll call him in the morning and tell him no."

"I'm sorry," Mandie said. "I know how much we need the money."

"We need the money. We don't need to be fools to get it." He pulled her close. "Thank you for seeing what I didn't want to see."

Dan called Raymond the next morning. He kept it simple: "We appreciate the offer, but we've decided to keep distribution in-house for now."

There was a beat of silence. When Raymond spoke again, the warmth was gone from his voice. "You're making a mistake, Dan. This market won't wait for you."

"I understand. Best of luck to you."

Raymond hung up without saying goodbye.

Dan set down the phone and looked at the plaque on the refrigerator. He'd made the right call. He was sure of it. But the mortgage deadline hadn't moved, and eight thousand dollars had just walked out the door.

#

"December 1st, ten minutes to closing, and I'm only half-dead. Things are looking up." Dan muttered to himself, watching the dwindling mall traffic. He resisted the urge to start packing away inventory. Twenty figurines sold today, plus his first internet order—his best day yet. The closest had been nineteen sales the day after Thanksgiving. His daily average hovered around twelve units. Though below their target, he hoped end-of-season sales would surge enough to reach their goal. He couldn't face Mandie and the kids if they lost their home. Those sales targets weren't just numbers anymore.

The experience brought mixed emotions. He loved selling items crafted by his own hands, cherished seeing the joy his figurines brought people. *I love what I do and I'm serving others*, he thought.

Dan reflected on his teachers, sensing he was on the right path. The Tree seemed closer each day. But the consequences of falling short would be devastating. That thought spurred him to action...

Dan gathered his things and headed for the exit. The sales were strong, but the math was unforgiving. Without additional revenue, they'd fall short of what they needed for the mortgage. He'd have to work longer hours—more figurines before the mall opened, more after it closed. Every piece he could produce was money toward saving the house.

Dan decided to contact the mortgage company about buying more time.

Chapter Twenty-One

"Any luck?" Mandie asked as Dan lowered his phone. He'd been working up the mortgage company's chain of command, seeking someone who could provide answers. The kids had left for school. Dan and Mandie sat in the kitchen before his mall shift. It was December 15th, with the foreclosure sale scheduled for January 4th.

"They said a five-thousand-dollar partial payment might convince them to delay the sale thirty days."

"Might? They wouldn't guarantee it?" Mandie pressed.

"That's all I could get from them," Dan said.

"At least it's a possibility," Mandie said. "What would we lose? We need to catch up anyway. What about the modification?"

"They said without steady employment or two years of self-employment history, they couldn't approve. I'd need either a longer business track record or provable regular income."

"So we're out," Mandie said. "And they won't guarantee postponing the sale even with payment?"

"No," Dan said. "They want a letter explaining my plan to catch up and maintain payments, plus minimum five thousand dollars. Then they'll consider it."

"Do we have five thousand?" Mandie asked.

"You know we don't," Dan answered. "You're tracking the numbers. We could manage it by skipping this month's utilities and using the kids' Christmas money. Plus postponing the attorney's two-thousand-dollar payment until next year. At least that situation hasn't worsened – still just paperwork, though he maintains depositions are coming."

"This hurts," Mandie said.

Dan's heart ached, but he struggled to maintain strength for Mandie.

"You're confident in the kiosk projections?"

"Based on current kiosk averages and the internet orders picking up, I project we can close most of the gap. Combined with Paul's final seasonal order, we should get close—but it'll be tight. Internet orders are increasing too—averaging five daily. Can't predict post-Christmas volume though."

"Alright," Mandie said. "So we have a chance to save the house. We sacrifice Christmas and delay utilities, but catch up before disconnection using incoming funds from kiosk and internet sales.""

"Paul's next payment is due in January. That plus continued daily sales should cover us."

"So if we make the payment now, it applies to the mortgage balance?"

"And accumulated late fees and penalties," Dan said.

"Which we'd owe anyway to save the house," Mandie noted.

"Yes," Dan agreed.

"Then let's proceed," Mandie said. "We need to keep our home."

"Agreed," Dan said. "Would you draft the letter? I need to focus on inventory."

"At least that's a good problem – needing more stock," Mandie said. "Reassure me again about projected sales."

"We've reached our target average for the season, with nine prime selling days remaining. Maintaining this rate puts us ahead. In short, It'll be close."

"But still insufficient to catch up on the house with kiosk sales alone?"

"About four thousand short after paying the five thousand," Dan said. He'd analyzed every possible scenario. Success hinged on maintaining the current pace and the internet orders continuing to grow. They were racing against time. That's why they needed to postpone the foreclosure sale that had been scheduled for just after the first of the year.

His figurines had proven successful, but financial stress tainted that victory. He could taste the tree's fruit, but it had soured. The price of success felt overwhelming. That would change if they succeeded. Dan realized success wasn't about the figurines – it was about providing for his family. Loving his work was wonderful, but his family needed his service most right now.

Chapter Twenty-Two

Dan gathered himself before opening the kiosk on December 17th, the season's home stretch. Despite his stress, he felt oddly optimistic. They'd submitted their letter and payment to the mortgage company, hoping for the best. They'd done everything possible – now events would unfold as they would. He and Mandie agreed they were due for good fortune after their string of setbacks.

Then customers began arriving. Usually mornings allowed time for creating figurines. Today brought steady traffic, yielding thirty-five sales – a new record. Though tired, Dan felt satisfied until realizing he hadn't produced a single new piece. He faced several hours of work at home just to replenish stock. The kiosk's inventory was thinning noticeably.

"Only another week until Christmas. I can manage until then," he told himself.

#

Another day had been long but fruitful, and Dan was glad it was over. He began opening storage bins to pack away product when he noticed a young man examining his work.

"Can I help you?" Dan asked.

The youth appeared eighteen or nineteen, wearing a canvas jacket over a black t-shirt and jeans. Dirty-blonde hair fell just past his ears and eyes.

"I really like your work," he said. "How long does each take?" He lifted a piece, studying it closely.

Dan was exhausted. The mall was closing. The young man showed no signs of buying, and Dan had answered this question countless times from curious but non-purchasing browsers. This felt like another such conversation.

"About fifteen minutes once you know the process. You cut and shape the pieces, then solder them together. The challenge is the initial design – determining the look. After that, it's like assembling a model." The explanation flowed automatically now.

"What gauge solder for the joints?"

"Ten."

"How do you bend without marking?"

"Trade secret, kid," Dan said, forcing a smile despite his fatigue. He aimed for politeness while avoiding a lengthy discussion. Too much remained to do before he could rest.

"Sorry, but I need to close. Got more work tonight. Stop by tomorrow during business hours and I'll answer your questions, okay?"

"Sure," the kid said, "Need help?"

Dan considered. "Why not? Help me pack up and lock down, and you can choose a figurine for your trouble."

"Thanks!" The youth entered the kiosk and began assisting.

He worked efficiently and pleasantly. Afterward, Dan thanked him and let him select a figurine. The young man wandered off as Dan eyed the cash drawer.

The bank meant a detour. Dan desperately needed to start production. Should he leave the cash overnight? His biggest sales day had produced mostly credit card transactions. Still...

Sighing deeply, he secured the cash box under his arm. He'd count at home and deposit in the morning. This way he'd save time while avoiding overnight risk.

Dan walked wearily through the mall toward his parking entrance, unaware of the young man watching his departure, then slipping back inside as Dan's car left the lot.

Chapter Twenty-Three

The first warning sign was an open storage bin beneath the kiosk. Dan didn't remember leaving it that way, but exhaustion had clouded last night's closing. He felt even more drained this morning after three hours crafting figurines and rising early for the bank deposit. Setting down his box of new pieces, he stepped over to investigate. As he slid the bin fully open, realization struck – it was empty!

Panic rising, he turned to the other bins. None of their locks were set. He yanked each door open, finding nothing but empty space. He'd been robbed!

#

Two hours later, Dan sat in the mall manager's office. Cody Braithwaite, a professional woman in her thirties, projected nervous energy from behind her oak desk.

"Mr. Benjamin, I've contacted the police. They'll arrive shortly. I've also pulled our security logs, and the officer on duty will report in person." Her nervousness intensified as she folded her hands over the black security log.

"According to the log, a young man – the same one who helped you close last night – showed our security officer a letter supposedly from you, authorizing him to remove inventory to make way for fresh stock this morning. He also presented what appeared to be a key to your storage bins. The officer had no reason to doubt the documentation or story."

"I never gave any such permission." Dan felt numb. They needed these kiosk sales to save their home. Without quick resolution, they'd lose everything – the house and their hopes. Why had he ever thought he could succeed? Why did every attempt meet such resistance? Everything in his life had crumbled except his marriage and family.

He dreaded telling Mandie. Maybe this would finally break her faith in him. He wouldn't blame her.

Ms. Braithwaite continued, "Pending the police investigation, you're released from your lease if you choose. We'll waive outstanding rent and refund all payments, including your deposit."

Dan looked up from studying his hands. "I can't continue. They took everything except what's in this box." He gestured to the cardboard container at his feet. *How do I tell Mandie*? He fought back tears. *Great – crying in front of the mall manager*. Still, the defeat crushed him. Nothing left to do... wait!

"Did I hear correctly?" he asked. "You'll refund everything?"

"Yes," Ms. Braithwaite said, her expression brightening slightly. "Given our security's involvement, the owners feel it's appropriate. I've ordered a check from corporate for $2,079. It should arrive within a week."

"Thanks," Dan said. The amount would help, but fell far short of their needs.

Ms. Braithwaite hesitated before continuing. "According to the log, the officer helped transfer inventory to their truck in exchange for two figurines." She rushed on, "This violated policy completely. The officer faces disciplinary action."

Uncomfortable silence fell. Dan had no words, and the manager seemed braced for his anger. He didn't have the energy. The situation's absurdity almost made him smile.

Noting his expression, the manager looked more alarmed. She produced a document. "To release your check, I just need your signature here." She slid the paper forward.

Dan scanned it quickly. It released the mall from liability and prevented legal action. His smile widened at the irony.

He could hear his attorney explaining how a lawsuit would drag on for months, requiring proof of negligence, arguments over inventory value, eventual insurance settlement. Dan understood the process now from his current legal battle. His involvement in that suit would probably count against him here – they'd suggest he orchestrated this to sue the mall.

"Get me the check first then I'll sign," Dan said, returning the document. She looked relieved though still nervous.

"We deeply regret this incident," she said. Dan sensed genuine sentiment.

"Me too," Dan replied. Mental calculations spun: $3,500 in lost inventory, likely loss of their home, and who knew what else would follow.

Just then a police detective was ushered into the office to take Dan's statement and begin the investigation.

Chapter Twenty-Four

Dan couldn't face home yet. Mandie would be at work anyway. He wandered the city Commons where everything had started – working with Paul, discovering he could earn from his figurines. The park stood empty except for occasional joggers sharing the path. They smiled and nodded as they passed. Dan forced return smiles.

Dan resumed walking. Hope wasn't completely extinguished. But nearly.

"You can't be serious!" Mandie exclaimed at Dan's news. "Everything's gone? They took it all?" She collapsed onto their front room couch.

Dan had sent Dan Jr. and the younger kids to a friend's house down the street. They didn't need to witness this conversation.

"I can't believe it! Every effort ends in disaster." Mandie dissolved into tears. Dan held her as she sobbed. Eventually she quieted, having moved closer rather than away as he'd feared.

"So we lose the house," Mandie said when she could speak. Dan's own eyes filled watching her pain. Her love for their home ran deep.

"I'm trying everything I can to save it. Paul's next payment and whatever I can produce and sell—it may not be enough, but I'm not giving up."

"You think that's possible?"

"It's worked before," Dan said. "Plus we haven't heard from the mortgage company. They might still delay the sale."

"No chance," Mandie said, anger edging her voice. "I didn't want to tell you, but they called this morning. Being so close to the sale date, they won't postpone. A letter's coming, but they wanted us informed. Only full payment stops the auction. They certainly didn't delay depositing our five thousand though. I checked – it's cleared."

"When did they call?" Dan asked.

"After you left this morning. I wanted you to have one good mall day before more bad news. Hah! So much for that. A good day at the mall." Mandie's laughter transformed into fresh tears. "Why is this happening to us?"

Dan had no answer.

Chapter Twenty-Five

The next morning, Dan dragged himself from bed. Mandie had already shepherded the kids off to school and left for work. She'd grown quiet after her initial breakdown, even after the children returned home. They hadn't spoken, even in bed. What remained to say? She seemed resigned, merely going through motions.

Dan recognized the same in himself. He showered, dressed, and headed to the garage to work on figurines—pure habit now.

What had begun as therapy had evolved into hope for a new life. Now that work felt like an albatross around his neck.

Perhaps if he hadn't chased this dream, he'd have secured another job by now. The mortgage company might be working with him on postponing the sale and modifying the loan.

Why had he been so foolish, pursuing a mere dream? "AAAAHHHRRRR!!!"

He sat at his workbench, staring into space, mind numb, emotions raw. Then the phone rang.

"Hello," Dan answered.

"Hey Dan, it's Benny. Just noticed something at Partridges—they've got a display that looks like your figurines. But checking closer, it's not your company name. It's Chandler's Designs. Did you change names, or have you got competition?"

Dan's stomach plummeted. "No, the company's still Dan's Designs."

"That's what I thought. Must be knockoffs then. Not even original with the name. Figure if they're copying your designs, might as well steal the name too. Thought you should know."

"Thanks, Benny," Dan said and hung up. His grip tightened on the phone. He wanted to smash it against the bench, but restraint won—phones cost money. A better idea struck. Dan jumped up, started the car as the garage door lifted, and sped away.

#

Dan entered Partridges, a well-known local gift shop. There sat the display—professional, well-lit, stocked with figurines that looked exactly like his. "Chandler's Designs" read the small placard at the base.

Chandler. Raymond Chandler. The man Dan had turned down weeks ago.

Dan lifted a figurine, examining it closely. His mark—the small crease on the right foot—was missing. He checked another. Also unmarked. He inspected every piece. Only three bore his signature mark—the ones that had been stolen from his kiosk.

The timeline assembled itself with sickening clarity. Raymond had approached Dan at the kiosk, watching him work, studying his product. Dan and Mandie had turned him down. Then the curious young man had appeared—asking detailed questions about the process, the gauge of solder, the bending technique. The youth had helped Dan close up, earned a free figurine to study, and then slipped back inside after Dan left.

The robbery that night. Every piece of inventory, gone.

And now—three weeks later—figurines appearing in stores under Raymond's name. Some with Dan's mark, stolen from the kiosk. The rest without it—copies, made by the youth Raymond had sent to learn Dan's craft.

Raymond hadn't offered Dan a business deal. He'd been scouting him. And when Dan said no, Raymond simply took what he wanted.

Dan stood in the gift shop, holding a figurine that wasn't his but *was* his, and felt a cold, clarifying anger. Not the helpless rage of the robbery. Something sharper. Mandie had been right about Raymond from the first moment. *Something feels wrong*, she'd said in the dark. Elizabeth's lesson, working through his wife's instincts. They'd done the right thing by saying no. And Raymond had punished them for it.

Dan set the figurine down carefully, walked out of the store, and retrieved his phone and the police detective's card from his jacket. He had solid leads on both the robbery and a new crime to report.

Chapter Twenty-Six

December 21st arrived. After the kids left for school, Mandie prepared for work. She wrapped her arms around Dan at the kitchen table. "You okay?"

"No," Dan responded flatly.

"I'm sorry this is crushing you," Mandie said, sitting and taking his hand. "I know you've given everything possible. At least the mall refund arrived – something to sustain us. I wanted to keep this house, but I've been thinking. It's just a building. And with the new relocation assistance program, we'll have another month or two."

Dan marveled at Mandie's transformed attitude. "What's happened? I can't believe you're not still angry, not calling me every kind of fool for such stupidity."

"We're both under a lot of pressure. Paul warned it would be harder than expected," Mandie reminded.

"Yes, but not this hard," Dan said. "It's impossible. If everyone faces this starting a business, it's amazing anyone tries. And I believed in a stupid dream!"

"It wasn't stupid!" Mandie insisted. "It was beautiful, and we gave everything. It could still succeed. People love your figurines – they sold wonderfully. Without the theft, you'd have triumphed!"

"Fat lot of good that does now," Dan said. "Even if I continue, peak season's over. Just small internet orders and occasional sales through Paul. We can't survive on that."

"No, but you can follow Ray's model. Sell to stores, develop contacts. Build gradually, even part-time. Find work and do this on the side until next season when you can expand. At least we know what to avoid now." Mandie smiled, trying to coax a response.

"The dream lives." She took his other hand. "Remember the dream's valley?"

Dan nodded.

"We're just still in the valley. Remember crawling on hands and knees for that final climb to the tree? We're that close. Don't surrender now. Maybe not this season, but others will come. I sense we'll succeed. We just need to stay on course."

Mandie kissed him. "We have the right recipe. You've proven that. We just need faith until it happens. And it will!"

Dan smiled and pulled her close.

"You'd make an excellent coach. Best pep talk ever. I'm still amazed by your change though. I thought you'd never forgive me. What transformed you?"

"I finally realized the house didn't create my happiness. Being with you and the kids did. When I released my grip on the building and understood we'd survive moving, still together as a family, I found peace.

"It took time, as you saw." Mandie winked. "But I've accepted it. The journey's longer than we hoped, but we'll reach our goal. My faith in you remains strong. You've worked harder than anyone I know. I couldn't ask more. You're not lazy – you're industrious, smart, and capable. You just need time. I'm giving it to you."

Tears filled Dan's eyes as he embraced her again. "I keep saying this, but you married far beneath yourself."

"No," Mandie said. "This *is* going to work."

Chapter Twenty-Seven

Dan sat at his garage workbench, uncertain what to do. It was the last day before Christmas break – the kids and Mandie would be at school until afternoon. Habit had drawn him here, but now he questioned whether to simply take time off. Nothing he accomplished today would significantly alter their immediate future.

Creating figurines used to transport him, offering precious moments when he felt his work held meaning, bringing joy to others. Somewhere amid the stress and pressure to produce, he'd lost that simple pleasure in designing and building.

Without conscious thought, his hands began gathering wire, molding shapes, collecting nuts and washers, soldering connection points. Inspiration guided him, and he watched with interest to see what would emerge.

Time dissolved as he worked. When complete, Dan cradled the figurine, tears welling as he studied it. His inner pain had found expression.

"I'll call this one The Beaten Man," Dan said aloud.

Though the title suggested defeat, something in the hunched figure still conveyed pride, determination, an unbroken will to survive.

Dan smiled. He'd created a self-portrait. Whether others would recognize it didn't matter – he saw it, and that made all the difference. Yes, he'd been beaten down, but hadn't surrendered.

He lost track of time studying the piece until his phone rang.

"Dan?"

"Hello Paul. Good to hear from you."

"Dan, I heard about the kiosk situation. Mandie filled me in. Sounds like you've hit some rough patches."

"That's putting it mildly," Dan said.

"Don't be too hard on yourself," Paul said. "You don't know this, but I had several rough patches starting out. Nearly went broke that first year, and not much better the second. It's part of learning. But in the future, call anytime. I'm never too busy for questions and moral support. You need to realize you really have something here."

"Thanks, Paul. I really appreciate all your help and encouragement." Dan settled into his desk chair.

"Listen, Dan. From what Mandie says, you were succeeding in a subpar mall. That's impressive. The figurines are clearly popular – they're selling well through my outlets. You can't quit now. I understand the urge to give up, but don't. You've already proven the concept. You just need to recover from this setback and learn from it. I still make mistakes. Press forward. Things will improve."

"Funny you should call now. I was just talking myself into getting back in the saddle." Dan recalled his response to the 'Beaten Man' figurine.

"Perfect timing," Paul said. "Because this isn't just a pep talk. I have a friend who runs several coastal fishing lodges and belongs to an association. He saw your fishing figurine and wants to discuss a line of fishermen for his gift shops. He thinks his association contacts will want them too. Not sure of the volume, but together they represent about fifty gift shops and lodges nationwide. Interested?"

Dan's breath caught. "You bet I'm interested!"

"Here's his number. Call him. I'll take ten percent commission on the first three orders for the referral. Fair?"

"More than fair," Dan said.

"Got to run. Hang in there. You've got a winner if you don't give up."

"I'd already decided to continue," Dan said, "but thanks for calling. It confirms I haven't lost my way. I'll keep pushing forward... And Paul. Thanks!"

"Don't mention it, buddy."

Dan sat contemplating after hanging up. Fifty gift shops. If each took two figurines initially, that meant a hundred-piece first order. Monthly reorders at that level... He caught himself. "Don't count sales before checks clear," he muttered. Still, it offered promising off-season business.

He booted his ancient laptop to check internet orders. Christmas shipping deadlines had passed, slowing orders, but curiosity drove him.

The computer clicked and whirred to life. His admin page showed three orders. He noted them for today's shipping. *Money still trickles in.*

Checking email next, his eyes widened. "What's this?"

The message came from Jordan Cranston, buyer for Woodman's Drug Stores: "Mr. Benjamin. Our local manager brought your figurines to my attention. He wants to stock them. After reviewing your website, I'd like to carry your products in all our stores. Got your email through the site. Please call to discuss our order." A phone number followed.

Dan's jaw dropped. He printed the email, fearing it might vanish. Research revealed Woodman's operated 357 stores throughout California, Oregon, Washington, and Montana. Quick calculations: five figurines per store meant 1,750 pieces, roughly $15,000. He reminded himself to breathe.

Payment timing seemed unlikely to save their house, but regular orders could provide sustainable income. Again, he forced calm. *Just make the call*, he told himself.

Chapter Twenty-Eight

"Hello. Mr. Cranston? Dan Benjamin here, regarding your email about stocking our figurines."

"Yes, Mr. Benjamin. Thanks for calling."

"My pleasure, sir. Please, call me Dan."

"Thanks, Dan. I'll be direct. I've shown your product to our buying committee. We want to test it chain-wide. Though we've missed Christmas, we see potential for post-holiday sales and smaller occasions. We'd like inventory in place before Valentine's Day. We've identified five figurines for testing."

"That sounds wonderful," Dan said, listening intently. He couldn't risk misunderstanding. This account could make their year.

"We're looking at two each of five figurines per store. Usually we test in limited clusters, but we're confident about your products. We want to capitalize on Valentine's Day."

Dan nearly choked when the numbers registered. "To confirm – ten figurines per store, and you have how many locations?" He knew but needed official confirmation.

"Currently 357 stores, so 3,570 figurines total. Two each of five designs. After testing, we'll likely expand the line if performance meets expectations. Would you consider our buyers' suggestions for new designs?"

"Absolutely," Dan fought to steady his voice as calculations raced through his mind. Hope flickered in his chest, and he reached for it.

"That's... substantial," Dan ventured carefully. "I'll need to order supplies. Any possibility of an advance for materials?"

"Standard terms are net thirty. Since you're new, I can authorize twenty percent advance if we shift to regular terms next time?"

"That works," Dan said, head spinning, heart pounding, barely believing this conversation.

"Excellent. We like your price point. Thinking standard keystone markup. That acceptable?"

Having worked with Paul, Dan understood immediately. He'd receive half retail – $10 per figurine. Perfect!

He drew a steadying breath before responding. "I can manage that, provided shipping goes to one address." His business mind engaged, remembering how secondary expenses could impact large orders.

"Standard procedure for this category," Jordan said. "Address will be on the purchase order, coming by email shortly. Sign, scan, and return it. Check arrives in about a week. We need delivery by January 31st latest. Feasible?"

Dan sat processing the implications.

"Dan?"

"Yes, sorry – I can do that." He wasn't certain, but 3,570 pieces? He'd make it work!

"Great," Jordan said. "Looking forward to working together. Think you've got something special here."

"Thanks!" Dan ended the call.

He sat motionless until his computer pinged – the purchase order arriving.

He printed, signed, scanned, and returned it immediately.

Then Dan grabbed his calculator, running numbers. His throat tightened as tears formed. He reached for his phone and began making calls...

#

"We're not losing the house?" Mandie's eyes widened, her jaw dropping. "Are you serious? How?" She and Dan sat on their worn living room couch. She'd left school early as usual, ensuring she'd be home before the kids.

Dan shared the day's revelations – Paul's call, then with renewed enthusiasm, described the Woodman's email and subsequent conversation.

"Bottom line," Dan said, "the Woodman's order brings in thirty-five thousand dollars. Their deposit arrives next week – seven thousand in cash! We already have most supplies from Christmas preparation, so we can bring the house current! I contacted the mortgage company and forwarded the purchase order. After review, the supervisor emailed just before you arrived. The sale's postponed thirty days!"

"You're not teasing?" Mandie sat straighter, searching Dan's eyes. "This isn't some cruel joke?"

"Not remotely. I checked with Paul – he says Woodman's is reliable. He also confirmed their purchase order constitutes a binding contract in retail. We're as secure as possible. Plus, we have thirty days to handle any complications."

"Am I dreaming? This is real?"

"I know the feeling. I've had longer to process it, but yes – it's absolutely real!"

Mandie melted into Dan's arms as they sat embracing, time suspended.

Dan reached into his back pocket and pulled out his wallet. He opened it and looked at the folded note behind his driver's license—Mandie's handwriting, seven words, creased and softened from a year of being carried. He'd looked at it a thousand times. This was the first time it felt like enough. He thought of Elizabeth—the woman who had refused to give him the answer because she loved him too much to make it easy. She had been right about everything. The arriving was the whole thing. In his mind, Dan stood at the Tree's base, fruit raised to his lips. It tasted exactly as sweet as he remembered.

Chapter Twenty-Nine

December 27th found Dan in the garage, tackling new orders. Meeting deadlines would require nearly round-the-clock work. Fortunately, he'd streamlined production to five minutes per piece by working assembly-line style on single designs. Paul's fishing contact had ordered 350 pieces with promises of more. Busy days ahead!

As he worked, Dan contemplated operational improvements. He could outsource nameplate engraving and mounting. If pressed, Mandie and Dan Jr. could help with assembly and soldering, or he might hire assistance. The process wasn't complex – the designs held the magic.

Remembering the youth's counterfeits and their near-accuracy made him wonder about the police investigation. He'd almost forgotten it amid recent developments.

Mandie appeared then.

"Can you come inside? We have a visitor."

Dan followed her to find the police detective in their front room.

"Please, sit," Dan gestured.

"This won't take long, Mr. Benjamin. Just updating you on the case."

Dan nodded. "I was just wondering about that." He felt Mandie slip her arm around his waist. She hadn't stopped smiling since learning about the house.

"We've arrested your Raymond Chandler and his young associate. Chandler's real name is Chadwick Bybee – a repeat offender. We found some of your inventory in his basement where the kid was producing copies. Several bore your mark, which proved crucial.

"During separate questioning," the detective continued, "the youth, faced with mall security footage, accepted a deal. He'll plead guilty and testify against Bybee. With his testimony plus yours, it's ironclad."

"Excellent news," Dan said. Mandie beamed beside him, joy radiating.

"What about our inventory?" Dan asked, thinking of pending orders. "When can we recover it?"

"Should be about a week. We'll retain some for evidence, but the rest is yours."

"Perfect!" Dan exclaimed. After endless setbacks, everything seemed to align. He gazed down at Mandie, heart swelling.

"You followed the recipe and solved the equation. Success was inevitable," she said.

"Excuse me, Ma'am?" The detective reached for his notebook.

"Just an inside reference, detective," Mandie waved dismissively, smiling. Then realization dawned. "What about store accounts? There's inventory in shops – and their sales. How do we handle that?"

Dan started, impressed. He'd focused on new business that saved their home. Mandie pursued full recovery.

"Well," the detective considered, "that likely requires court proceedings."

"Taking months," Mandie said. "Meanwhile, we have operations to maintain."

Dan blinked back joyful tears, throat tight watching Mandie's earnestness. She'd fully embraced their *venture*. She too had tasted the Tree's fruit.

Again, he thanked providence for bringing them together. His love deepened daily, growing exponentially through their trials. The fruit tasted sweeter for sharing it.

"Could we meet the prosecutor?" Mandie asked. "I have an idea to strengthen your case..."

#

"Ready for final totals?" Mandie asked Dan at their kitchen table. January 14th had arrived. Recent weeks brought whirlwind activity beyond Dan's production and shipments.

Mandie had assumed responsibility for paperwork and "loss recovery," as she termed it. Her business coursework had prepared her for exactly this kind of work—invoicing, collections, financial tracking. What had started as self-improvement had become the operational backbone of their business.

Two days after the detective's visit, they'd met with the prosecutor to implement Mandie's strategy. She proposed that if Bybee relinquished all records, billings, and store inventory claims, plus cooperated with collections, they'd drop fraud charges. He'd face only the mall theft, plead guilty, and receive reduced sentencing. It was the kind of deal structure she'd studied in her coursework—a negotiated resolution that gave both sides a reason to cooperate. The prosecutor, accustomed to lengthy fraud cases, looked at her with visible surprise.

Since fraud carried the heaviest penalties, Bybee readily agreed to avoid prison. He provided everything requested. The prosecutor appreciated the guilty plea and swift case resolution.

Mandie's invoices to stores included court documentation confirming legal ownership, ensuring prompt payment to Dan's Designs.

"Remember, these are net figures after expenses," Mandie noted. "We've received nine thousand five hundred forty-two dollars from stores."

Dan held his breath as she continued.

"Two thousand seven hundred ten from Paul's orders."

Dan swallowed hard.

"And you'll clear twenty-six thousand nine hundred seventy-five from Woodman's after deducting deposit and shipping."

Dan swept Mandie up, spinning her in an embrace. "This is incredible!"

"Don't forget your fishing connection," Mandie said once her feet touched ground. "His three thousand five hundred arrives within seven days.

"Combined with festival and kiosk earnings, that's forty-four thousand nine hundred seventy-five dollars total!"

"Unbelievable!" Dan exclaimed.

"Better yet, repeat orders continue year-round." Mandie's eyes sparkled. "Congratulations, my love. You've earned more in six months than ever before. And that's just startup phase. Sales will grow. We can officially declare this business successful!" She clasped Dan's hands.

"Your dream has come true!"

Dan's heart thundered as words failed him. He gazed at Mandie. She too was speechless.

Chapter Thirty

Dan stood on the sidewalk outside the attorney's office, blinking in the afternoon sun. The door had closed behind him. The last document had been signed. It was over.

He stood there for a long moment, letting it settle. A year of legal threat, of FBI interviews, of sleepless nights wondering whether Contra Pro's collapse would take more than just his savings—it would take his name. And now a man in a suit had shaken his hand, said "You're clear," and sent him out into the sunlight.

He called Mandie from the parking lot.

"It's over," he said.

Silence on the line. Then Mandie's breath, long and unsteady, as if she'd been holding it for months. "Come home," she said.

When Dan walked in, Mandie was on the couch with their copy of what they'd begun calling The Opportunity Tree Dream. So much had transpired since that night. He hung his coat in the closet and settled beside her.

"The FBI determined I had no management responsibilities over the finances," he said. "That cleared the criminal investigation, and the attorney confirmed the last civil filings are dropped. It's all behind us now." He draped an arm around Mandie's shoulders. "Another nightmare laid to rest."

"Speaking of dreams," Mandie said, turning toward him. She held up the highlighted pages. "Nearly everything in yours has come to pass. The path, the tree, the side trails, the valley—we've lived through all of it."

Dan nodded. He'd thought the same thing many times. But hearing Mandie say it aloud, in their living room, with the worst of it behind them—it felt different now. It felt true in a way it hadn't before.

"There's one part I keep coming back to," Mandie said. "The man in the boat. He floated up to the tree, tasted the fruit, shrugged, and left. He didn't value it because it cost him nothing."

Dan was quiet for a moment.

"You're saying that's what the struggle was for," he said. "Not punishment. Preparation. If we'd gotten here easily, we might have shrugged too."

"Exactly." Mandie squeezed his hand. "I'm grateful we didn't give up. That *you* didn't give up. What matters is that we persevered, and we value what we've gained."

"But the dream continues. Remember when you left the canyon to plant another tree from the saved seeds?"

"I remember," Dan said, warmth filling his heart at the memory.

"What do you think it means? That part hasn't manifested yet."

"What it means, dear heart," Dan pulled Mandie close, "is that our adventure is far from complete..." Mandie smiled and reached for her manila folder on the side table. She opened it to a page near the back, and Dan saw something he hadn't noticed before—a small piece of blue silk, no bigger than a handkerchief, tucked between the pages like a bookmark. Elizabeth's first fabric. The swatch Michael had given Mandie the day she'd visited him alone, carrying a promise from a woman who was already gone. Mandie touched the silk lightly, then closed the folder. "She'd be proud of us," Mandie said quietly. "I think she'd say we walked on rough ground. And we didn't stop."

Mandie set the folder aside and stood. She crossed to the kitchen, took a piece of paper from the junk drawer, and found a pen. Dan followed her and leaned against the doorframe, watching.

She stood at the counter beneath the wooden plaque, studying the seven words she'd burned into it the day she'd folded the original note into Dan's wallet. Then, in her careful hand, she wrote a single line on the paper and taped it beneath the plaque:

Follow the Path, Live the Dream.

She stepped back. Dan came up behind her and wrapped his arms around her. They stood together, reading the plaque and its new companion in the kitchen light.

Invest your time. Don't just spend it.
Follow the Path, Live the Dream.

"That's it," Dan said quietly. "That's the whole thing."

Appendix
How to Grow an Opportunity Tree Workbook
*A Practical Guide to Finding and Growing Your
Opportunity*

A Note Before You Begin

If you've just finished How to Grow an Opportunity Tree, you've walked with Dan and Mandie through their darkest year — and watched them come out the other side with something they built with their own hands, their own time, and their own stubborn refusal to quit.

In Book One, Dan and Mandie discovered the Ultimate Investment: Time. In Book Two, they discovered what to do with it: find the work you love, follow the path, and tend the tree until it bears fruit.

This workbook takes the three core frameworks from the story — The Path, The Seed, and The Recipe — and gives you practical tools to apply them in your own life. If you completed the Book One workbook, this is the next step. If you haven't, start there — the principles build on each other.

Elizabeth's business notebook, the one Michael gave Mandie, was full of practical notes from a woman who was figuring things out as she went. Think of this workbook the same way. It's not a manual. It's a companion for the journey.

Let's begin.

Section One: The Path

Dan's dream showed him a path through a canyon to a magnificent tree. The path was clear but not easy. Side trails glittered with false promises. A valley obscured his view. The final climb was steep. But the path led where it promised, and those who walked it tasted fruit that those who arrived by boat could not appreciate.

The Path is a metaphor for your journey toward work you love. Here are the principles it teaches:

Stay on the Path

Every worthwhile pursuit will present side trails — shortcuts, get-rich-quick schemes, opportunities that glitter but have no substance. Dan and Mandie faced one in Raymond Chandler's offer: easy money, no contracts, too good to be true. They said no. The path is harder than the side trails, but it's the only one that leads to the tree.

> *Ask yourself: Am I on the path, or have I wandered onto a side trail? Is this opportunity real, or does it just sparkle?*

Expect the Valley

Every worthwhile endeavor includes at least one low point — times of struggle, toil, and desperate scraping by. These moments test your limits. This is where many surrender. You must decide if the end goal justifies the effort to persevere and climb the other side.

If you determine the reward won't merit the struggle, stop and redirect your energy. But if the end goal warrants it, double down, hold fast, and produce your finest work until you emerge from the valley.

The reward awaiting you is, as you already know, beyond price.

The Final Climb Is the Hardest

Dan's last thirty feet to the tree were the steepest. In life, the final push — the last stretch before breakthrough — is often the most grueling. Dan and Mandie nearly lost their home in the final weeks before the Woodman's order arrived. They kept climbing. Release things that don't truly matter. Cherish what's genuinely important — family and treasured relationships. And keep climbing.

Reflection: Where Are You on the Path?

Look at where you are right now. Be honest.

Am I on the path, or wandering the canyon floor?

Have I been tempted by a side trail? What was it?

Am I in the valley right now? What would it take to keep moving?

Section Two: The Seed

Blaine, the stuffed-animal maker, taught Dan that finding the right opportunity is like planting a seed. You must choose carefully, nurture patiently, and be honest about whether the seed is growing.

Here is the process Blaine outlined, adapted for your own use:

Step 1: Begin with an Idea

It's like a small seed. Gather a measure of faith and a deep desire for the seed to grow. Imagine the future of planting this seed. Does it align with your values and goals? Will you truly love it? Don't plant tomatoes if you dislike tomatoes. Only nurture what you believe you'll love.

Step 2: Test the Soil

Research your idea. Talk to people who have done something similar. Study the market, the costs, the requirements. Is the soil right for this seed? Dan discovered his figurines had commercial potential only after Mr. Shenk paid $20 for one and Paul saw them at the festival. Test before you commit everything.

Step 3: Plant and Nurture

Begin your journey. A strong seed continues growing. A weak one fades. As you work, ask yourself honestly: Do I still love this? Will it serve others? This proves most challenging. Carefully distinguish between seed quality and cultivation. If the soil is poor or nourishment inadequate, the gardener must improve. If the seed proves weak despite proper care, it's time to uproot it and plant something new.

Step 4: Tend with Faith and Patience

Faith, diligence, patience, and perseverance matter even with good seeds. Dan spent months making figurines before earning significant income. He worked temp jobs to survive while tending his seed. The harvest comes to those who tend — but it comes on its own schedule, not yours.

Step 5: Harvest

The harvest brings true delight, and planting the seeds of the right opportunity nourishes you for life. When you're doing what you love while serving others, it transcends mere work. It becomes a precious journey.

Your Seed Assessment

What idea or opportunity am I considering?

Does it align with what I truly love? (Be honest.)

Will it serve others? How?

What soil does it need? (Education, capital, practice, connections?)

Am I willing to tend this seed for months or years before harvesting?

Section Three: The Recipe

Mr. Shenk, Dan Jr.'s chemistry teacher, taught Dan that success follows a formula — just like chemistry, just like baking. If you want a specific result, you follow the recipe. Follow it correctly, and you'll get the desired result. It's a natural law.

Here is the recipe framework, adapted for building your opportunity:

1. Decide What You Want to Create

Be specific in your goal. What do you truly want? Not what sounds impressive or what others expect — what do you want? Dan wanted to make figurines. Not "start a business" in the abstract. Figurines. Specific, tangible, real.

2. Find the Right Recipe

Study those who have succeeded before you, or achieved something similar. Document your understanding. Dan learned from Blaine (the philosophy), Shenk (the formula), and Paul (the execution). Each teacher gave him one piece of the recipe. Expect adjustments along the way.

3. Gather the Right Ingredients

List what you need: education or skills, certifications if required, practice through trial and error, mentors and advisors, capital (however modest), and a market of people you can serve. Dan's ingredients were wire, solder, a workbench, Paul's mentorship, and fifteen years of customer knowledge.

4. Mix in Proper Order

Begin your journey. Follow the recipe you've discovered and documented. Dan didn't quit his temp jobs to make figurines full-time — he did both. He built inventory while earning income. Order matters.

5. Cook with Time

Apply the Ultimate Investment — Time — and allow completion through consistent effort, day after day, week after week. Eventually, you'll create something that nourishes you for life. Whether recipe, formula, or planting a seed, the principles remain constant. Strict adherence to the right process inevitably leads to success.

Your Recipe

What specific thing do I want to create or build?

Who has done something similar? What can I learn from them?

What ingredients do I need? (List everything.)

What is my order of operations? (What comes first, second, third?)

How much time am I willing to invest daily? Weekly?

Section Four: Three Keys for the Journey

Key 1: Meet Your Immediate Needs

Work however necessary to meet your immediate obligations. Dan loaded trucks. Mandie took a school aide job. There is no shame in doing what it takes to keep your family fed and housed while you build something better. The temp work isn't the destination — it's the bridge.

Key 2: Plan for Basic Security

Build a safety net, however small. Have a Plan B. Dan and Mandie kept a spreadsheet, tracked every dollar, and made hard choices about what they could and couldn't afford. Mandie's business coursework gave her the tools to manage their finances with precision. You don't need an MBA — you need awareness of where your money goes and a plan for keeping the lights on while you grow.

Key 3: Invest Incrementally

Use the incremental investing of your Time to move forward into something you truly love — with a plan. Not all at once. Not recklessly. Incrementally. Dan spent evenings in the garage. Mandie studied after the kids went to bed. Small deposits of time, compounded daily, built something neither of them could have imagined a year earlier.

Your Three Keys

Key	My Plan	By When
1. Immediate Needs		
2. Basic Security		
3. Incremental Investment		

Section Five: Your Plaque

Dan and Mandie's wooden plaque grew with them. In Book One, Mandie burned seven words into it: "Invest your time. Don't just spend it." At the end of Book Two, she taped a new line beneath it: "Follow the Path, Live the Dream."

Two lines. Two books' worth of wisdom. Simple enough to read every morning while pouring coffee. Deep enough to carry for a lifetime.

**Invest your time. Don't just spend it.
Follow the Path, Live the Dream.**

A Final Word

Dan's dream showed him a tree with golden fruit. The fruit was real. But the dream also showed him something subtler: the man in the boat who tasted the fruit, shrugged, and left. He didn't value it because it cost him nothing.

The struggle is not an obstacle to the reward. The struggle is what makes the reward worth having. Dan and Mandie didn't succeed because they were lucky or talented or had the right connections. They succeeded because they refused to stop walking the path when the valley got dark, when the side trails sparkled, when the final climb seemed impossibly steep.

Elizabeth knew this. She wrote in her business notebook: "The business will fail as many times as it needs to before it succeeds. My job is to outlast the failures."

Sheldon knew it too. He showed up at six in the morning with two thermoses of coffee, not because anyone asked him to, but because he couldn't not.

You know it now. The question is the same as it was at the end of Book One: What will you do with your time tomorrow morning?

Find the work you love. Serve others through it. Follow the path. Tend the tree. And when the fruit comes — and it will come — you will know exactly what it's worth, because you walked every step of the way to get there.

Invest your time. Don't just spend it.

Follow the Path, Live the Dream.

See how Dan and Mandie learn to handle their new success in the next episode:

Thinning Your Life

Work Less, Do More, Be Wealthy

About the Author:

H. Bradley Stucki was born and raised in the desert Southwest, keeping horses, cows, and other assorted pets. He is the third of 6 children and survived childhood only by utilizing an active imagination. His hobbies include reading and travel. He and his wife live in a high mountain valley with a population of 200.

See other works by H. Bradley Stucki at www.amazon.com/author/hbstucki. Free downloads are often available. Click "Follow" on his Author Page for updates on new releases.